COMMANDO
MEN

PEN & SWORD MILITARY CLASSICS

We hope you enjoy your Pen and Sword Military Classic. The series is designed to give readers quality military history at affordable prices. Pen and Sword Classics are available from all good bookshops. If you would like to keep in touch with further developments in the series, telephone: 01226 734555, email: enquiries@pen-and-sword.co.uk, or visit our website at www.pen-and-sword.co.uk.

Published Classics Titles

Forthcoming Titles

COMMANDO MEN

THE STORY OF
A ROYAL MARINE COMMANDO
IN WORLD WAR TWO

BRYAN SAMAIN

PEN & SWORD MILITARY CLASSICS

First published in Great Britain in 1988 by Greenhill Books
Published in 2005, in this format, by
PEN & SWORD MILITARY CLASSICS
an imprint of
Pen & Sword Books Limited
47 Church Street
Barnsley
S. Yorkshire
S70 2AS

Copyright © Bryan Samain, 1988, 2005

ISBN 1 84415 209 X

The right of Bryan Samain to be identified
as the Author of this Work has
been asserted by him in accordance with
the Copyright, Designs and Patents Act 1988.

A CIP record for this book
is available from the British Library.

Printed and bound in Great Britain by
CPI UK

Pen & Sword Books Ltd incorporates the imprints of
Pen & Sword Aviation, Pen & Sword Maritime, Pen & Sword Military,
Wharncliffe Local History, Pen & Sword Select,
Pen & Sword Military Classics and Leo Cooper

For a complete list of Pen & Sword titles please contact:
PEN & SWORD BOOKS LIMITED
47 Church Street, Barnsley, South Yorkshire, S70 2AS, England.
E-mail: enquiries@pen-and-sword.co.uk
Website: www.pen-and-sword.co.uk

CONTENTS

To
Lieutenant Peter Winston, and
all the other officers and men
of Commando Group, who
fought and died for an ideal

ILLUSTRATIONS

MAPS

PREFACE

LORD LOUIS MOUNTBATTEN once said in a broadcast speech that the general public's conception of a Commando soldier seemed to be something akin to a Chicago gangster, and that nothing could be farther from the case.

How right Lord Louis was. The men of the Commandos were ordinary men, drawn from all walks and creeds of life, who received special training for special tasks. Like their brothers-in-arms at Arnhem, they were not supermen —just ordinary men who had a job to do.

As everyone knows, the term 'Commando' was originally used by the Boers at the beginning of the century to describe their mounted bands of irregulars who played havoc with the supply columns of the British Army in South Africa. Since the recent war, however, the word has become a household one throughout the world. The Allied Commando organisation, although predominantly British, also had men from France, Belgium, Poland, America, Jugoslavia and Germany serving in its ranks.

Many people have asked me in the past exactly what a Commando—as we knew it during the war—consisted of. Briefly, it may be described as a self-supporting unit of some 450 to 500 men—roughly half an infantry battalion, that is—with a correspondingly smaller scale of transport and weapons of support, such as three-inch mortars and Vickers medium machine-guns.

The Commando units referred to in this book were divided into five fighting Troops of sixty men apiece, together with an Headquarters Troop and Heavy Weapons Troop. Forty-five Commando's fighting Troops were designated by the letters A (for Able), B (for Baker), C (for Charlie), D (for Dog), and E (for Easy). Other Commandos in the First Special Service Brigade used numbers instead of letters for Troop designations. Throughout the book, to avoid confusion as far as possible, I have referred to the fighting Troops of 45 Commando as Able Troop, Baker Troop, etc.

This book attempts to give some account of a Commando in action from D Day to VE Day in North-West Europe; but the deeds of this specific Commando are inextricably bound with those of its parent formation—First Special Service Brigade.* Therefore, if I have made but slight reference to the other three Commando units in the Brigade I can only apologise, and express the hope that they will also contribute their side of the common story we have to tell.

BRYAN SAMAIN

LONDON, 1948.

* Later renamed ' First Commando Brigade.'

ACKNOWLEDGMENTS

THE Author wishes to express his indebtedness to the following persons, without whose co-operation this book would not have been possible:

Commander T. Woodrooffe, R.N., Editor of *Dittybox*, the magazine of the Royal Navy, for permission to reproduce the Author's account of Lieutenant Peter Winston's adventures; the Editor of *The Globe and Laurel*, for permission to embody some of the Author's published articles, and for assistance with maps; the Central Office of Information, for kind assistance with photographs; and Mr. Walter Walker, for all the time and trouble taken in preparing maps to illustrate the narrative.

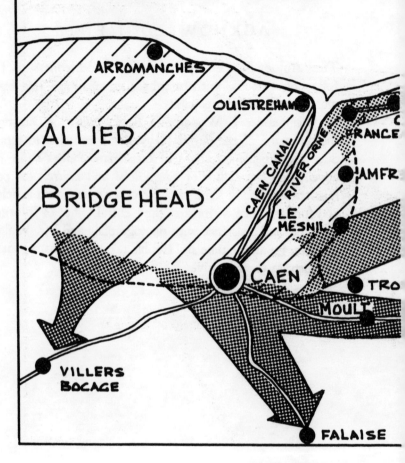

NORMANDY – THE BREAKOUT – Au

ARROMANCHES

OUISTREHAM

ALLIED

BRIDGEHEAD

CAEN CANAL

RIVER ORNE

FRANCE

AMFR

LE MESNIL

CAEN

TRO

MOULT

VILLERS BOCAGE

FALAISE

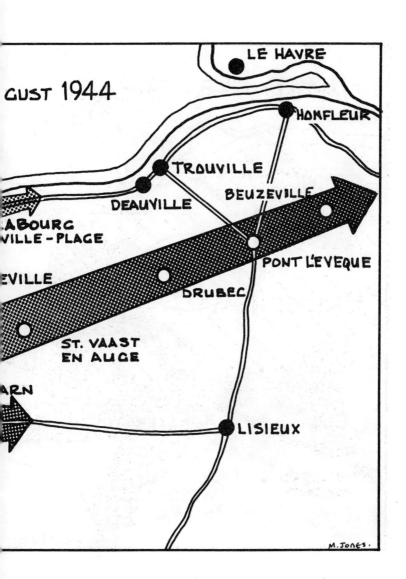

LE HAVRE

GUST 1944

HONFLEUR

TROUVILLE

BEUZEVILLE

DEAUVILLE

ABOURG
VILLE - PLAGE

PONT L'EVEQUE

EVILLE

DRUBEC

ST. VAAST
EN AUGE

ARN

LISIEUX

M. JONES.

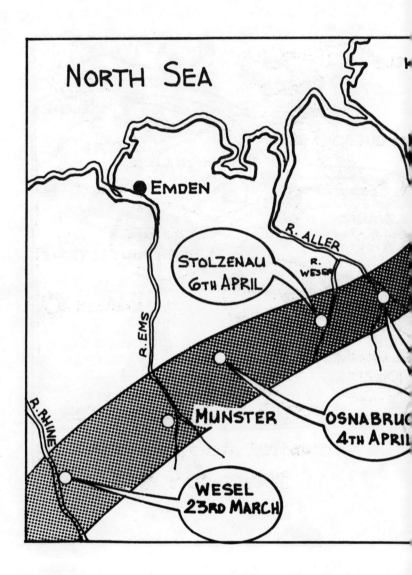

NORTH SEA

EMDEN

R. ALLER

R. WESER

STOLZENAU
6TH APRIL

R. EMS

R. RHINE

MUNSTER

OSNABRUC
4TH APRIL

WESEL
23RD MARCH

FIRST COMMANDO BRIGADE'S
ADVANCE ACROSS GERMANY
MARCH-MAY 1945

M JONES

PART ONE

NORMANDY

Chapter 1

D DAY—JUNE 6, 1944

THE sea was choppy in the English Channel. A vast armada of invasion craft battled unceasingly against the relentless swell, swaying and rocking as they strove to keep in line ahead and reach their objective.

On board the craft men tried to ease their aching, cramped limbs. They had been at sea for some hours now, and their faces were drawn with pain as they fought back the contents of their bellies, which threatened to retch up at any minute.

Someone passed round the rum. We all drank it, whether we really wanted to or not. Quite a few of us were on our way to becoming gloriously merry—if only our heaving stomachs would have let us.

The sea was all too distracting. We tried to concentrate and remember. We had a job to do. Our objective was Queen Red Beach, Normandy.

2

On the French coastline, a blurred grey strip in the distance, pin-prick flashes of guns determined the positions of heavy German shore batteries replying to our furious naval bombardment. The force supporting our particular

3

flotilla of landing craft included the battleships *Ramillies* and *Warspite,* the monitor *Roberts,* and a host of destroyers, all of which were busily engaging previously selected targets in the landing area.

The noise was deafening. The air was filled with the rumble of deadly gunfire, the eye-wracking flashes of salvoes barking viciously from the turrets of innumerable ships, and the shrill whine of shells hurtling towards the coast. Overhead, in the dull, louring sky, our air superiority was becoming more and more evident. Below the hundreds of bombers droning monotonously towards their objectives twin-tailed Lightning aircraft circled in a fussy manner, like anxious mothers keeping their children from danger.

We were nearing the beaches now : there was only about a mile or so to go. Suddenly, the first shells from German guns began to fall round our long, precarious column of craft. To port and starboard landing craft which had been hit were already blazing furiously, the seas showing only the bobbing heads of men who had jumped from them to escape the fury of the flames.

The run-in to Queen Road Beach commenced. Despite the swell, it was fairly smooth. Landmarks—so carefully studied on air photographs before we left the marshalling area at Southampton—could now easily be seen. Everyone looked to their weapons and ammunition, to their rifles and tommy-guns, to the bombs on their belts, and the fighting knives strapped to their hips. We checked our rucksacks, too, those heavy packs which held everything we needed to fight for three days without supplies from anyone, and which totalled anything up to eighty pounds in weight.

Our flotilla drew nearer the beach : two hundred yards to go. Those pin-prick flashes we had seen about twenty minutes before were now great gaping orange flashes, rending the heavens in angry reply to the merciless bombardment of the Royal Navy.

We were getting very close now. A few miles beyond the curtain of fire hanging over the German beach defences we could just see the mushroom-like explosions of heavy bombs dropped by the R.A.F. as they mingled with the frantic puffs of enemy gunfire.

The bottoms of our craft scraped ominously over treacherous underwater obstacles of wire and concrete as we covered the last fifty yards. Suddenly, a German battery of anti-tank guns opened up on us from a flank. Through the haze of thick smoke and the deafening roar of the battery—firing at almost point-blank range—someone was trying to shout orders. Men were scrambling furiously to obey, but no sooner had they leapt to their feet than they seemed to crumple visibly, fumbling with dazed, frightened hands for tender wounds.

There was a thunderous splash as the craft beached on the edge of the wreckage-filled water, in most cases still with four or five feet of water for'ard. Everyone began to pile out now, a furious, desperate collection of men in green berets, white teeth grinning viciously across blackened faces. Holding their precious weapons high above their heads they waded ashore, the cold salt water coming up to their chests, enveloping their heavy rucksacks, the soft, silky sand giving little support to their struggling feet.

The time was ten past nine in the morning. Forty-five Commando had landed.

3

The beach proved to be mined, and the enemy were putting up a desperate fight with everything they had.

Great coastal guns were raking successive waves of landing craft still coming in with more and more British troops, whilst German artillery some miles behind the beach-head area, supported by countless mortars and machine-guns, added to the general confusion.

Leaving casualties behind them the Commando raced up the beach towards First SS Brigade's check point, a small wood about one thousand yards inland.

Running desperately, our boots squelching with sea water, our clothes sodden, and the heavy rucksacks rubbing our shoulders sore, we made for the swamps which had to be crossed if we were to reach the wood—deep, thick swamps, almost impassable. Panting now, we eventually struggled through them, a great surging mass of men, eager not to be left behind in that first rush for the all-important check-point.

We had to reach the wood as quickly as possible, assemble as a Brigade, then move off again to fight our way across the River Orne, which lay to the east, beyond whose banks men of the Sixth Airborne Division had landed the night before, and were now fighting a bloody battle to hold their positions until we could reinforce them.

We sorted ourselves out into single file, to become a long, winding snake of men, each of us carrying heavy equipment of some sort or another. Some trudged with mortars or PIATs on their backs, others carried stretchers and extra-heavy medical rucksacks. A few even pushed bicycles. Of all things to go to war with, perhaps a bicycle was the worst.

By this time Number 6 Commando and elements of Brigade headquarters had already reached the wood, having landed before us. They were waiting for us to join them before moving on. Within half an hour we had done so, together with Number 3 Commando, whereupon Bryan White (our Adjutant) produced his hunting horn and solemnly blew ' Gone Away ' as a rally signal to stragglers who might still be on the beaches.

With most of the Brigade now having successfully reached the check-point and reorganised, everyone stood by for the advance to the Orne. There was a slight delay whilst 6 Commando tackled a German strong-point which tried to impede our progress, whilst from elsewhere the enemy opened fire with mortars. We all lay flat and very still as those small, yet deadly bombs whistled with disconcerting accuracy on to the wood. Fortunately the ground was very soft, so we suffered no casualties.

The enemy mortar fire lifted as suddenly as it started, and 6 Commando reported that they had succeeded in silencing the strong-point. We were still being shelled spasmodically, however, as we rose to our feet, picked up our weapons, and prepared to move off once again.

News was now received that the Brigade was to come under command of the Sixth Airborne Division, and that the 5th Parachute Brigade had captured their objectives— the bridges over the Orne and Caen canal—intact. The Brigade Commander, Lord Lovat, therefore decided to pass us over the bridges as soon as possible in order to link up with the Airborne troops.

The men of the Airborne Division had been hard pressed: there was no doubt about that. When, at a quarter past twelve that afternoon we finally crossed the bridges, we found them tired, grimy, but still cheery, after twenty-four hours' continuous fighting.

It was an historic meeting. The first inkling they had of our coming was the sound of Lord Lovat's piper playing a lilting Highland march as we advanced to meet them.

They cheered us, a ragged cheer, broken with the wicked chatter of machine-gun fire in the distance: and then, quite suddenly, we found ourselves among them. The green berets mingled with the red. . . .

Yes, it was a great moment; but we, for our part, had not got over the bridges without casualties. There had been a German sniper covering our particular bridge who had succeeded in picking off every alternate man with deadly accuracy. Machine-guns had harassed us from a flank, too.

Our most serious casualty at the hands of this sniper was our Commanding Officer, Lieutenant-Colonel N. C. Ries, R.M., wounded in the thigh. He had to be evacuated, and we heard later that he was wounded a second time whilst lying on a stretcher on the beaches, waiting to be taken off to a ship.

With the C.O. out of action our second-in-command, Major Nicol Gray, took over. His task was unenviable, since he had been thrust into command in the middle of a battle, with scant knowledge of how many men in the unit had survived the landing and the fighting so far. However, he proved more than equal to the task, and although we did not know it then, this was the man who was destined to lead us across Normandy, Holland, and Germany.

4

In the original landing plan 45 Commando's first task after crossing the Orne was to capture a certain heavily defended gun battery at Merville—providing such a capture had not already been achieved by the 9th Parachute Battalion of the Airborne Division.

We still did not know whether the gun battery was in enemy hands or not, for no word had been received from the paratroops. Lord Lovat therefore ordered us to advance to Merville and, if necessary, to capture the battery and the nearby coastal town of Franceville-Plage.

Within a matter of minutes we were again on the move, led by Charlie Troop—our cyclist Troop—and heading for Merville as rapidly as possible. Meanwhile, 6 Commando were commencing an attack on the German-held village of Le Plein, which stood on a small hill half a mile to the east.

The village of Salanelles—which lay between Le Plein and Merville—was reached by us without opposition. After passing down the main street Charlie Troop turned east at the far end, failing to leave anyone behind to guide the rest of us on.

As the leading men (which included Major Gray) neared the point where Charlie Troop had turned off they suddenly saw a group of Germans running across the road in front of them, about a quarter of a mile away, making for what seemed to be a strong-point.

Both the enemy and ourselves seemed to see each other at precisely the same time, opening fire with everything; but the former had the advantage. They had the road well and truly covered with numerous machine-guns, making all movement impossible. As a result, Major Gray's headquarter party and a section of Easy Troop following on behind were completely ' pinned down ' in a ditch at the side of the road, unable either to advance or retire.

After twenty minutes Major Gray finally decided to make a run for it, and rejoin the rest of the unit hidden from view in Salanelles. All those of his party who could move without being unduly exposed were ordered to crawl along the ditch leading to the village. The remainder had to make their way back as soon as they could, for we hadn't time to wait for them.

In the words of Major Gray, it was an extremely painful retreat. However, the bulk of his party (including himself) succeeded in rejoining the unit unscathed, although they were harassed the whole way back by enemy mortar and machine-gun fire.

Once back with the main body, the C.O. lost no time. He ordered our 3-inch mortars into action on the strong-point to cover our advance to Merville by a different route. The mortar crews were delighted. They had been carrying their heavy bombs and weapons ever since landing, and had not yet had a chance to use them. Under the supervision of Captain Bill Neaves they sent over thirty high-explosive bombs soaring into the German position in no time at all.

Whilst our mortars steadily rained fire down on the enemy, Major Gray took the rest of the Commando round on a flank, and thus eventually reached a large stretch of open ground to the north of the Merville Battery, which now lay between us and Franceville-Plage. No sooner had our leading element reached this open ground, however, than they were fired on by the Battery, as soon as they exposed themselves to view. Major Gray at once decided to attack.

But the assault on this formidable position was not to be. Whilst Major Gray was making his reconnaissance prior to the attack, a signal was received from Lord Lovat ordering 45 Commando to capture and hold Merville for the night, and not to advance to Franceville-Plage, as previously planned.

Ignoring the Battery, we set about clearing the village of Merville. This was not easily done, for there were a lot of Germans to be winkled out who were hiding in the oddest places, including the entire staff of a headquarters. By seven o'clock that evening, however, we were in full posses-sion of what was left of the village, for the R.A.F. had done some good work in this area before we arrived.

Once we knew the village to be ours we started to dig in as rapidly as possible, and within a matter of an hour or so the entire unit was safely ' underground ' in good, deep slit trenches, or ' slitters ' as we called them.

It was true that we had not been in Normandy very long—only a matter of hours, in fact. But already we had realised the value of digging. One of our men once said that all a soldier needed when he went into action was ' a bloody good rifle and a bloody good shovel,' which turned out to be true enough.

Our men knew how to dig, too. They had done it so many times during the past four years on exercises with the Royal Marine Division in England. One of the greatest exponents of the art serving with us was ' Digger ' Jordan, a young Marine who hailed from Easy Troop, commanded by Major Ian Beadle.

' Digger ' was no peacetime navvy: in fact, as far as we knew he had been a humble clerk in an office. But there was no doubt about it, when things started and the order came to dig, ' Digger ' would always be first down in a comfortable slit trench. His record was about fifteen minutes —in soft soil, of course.

Commando headquarters was established that night in two broken-down cottages in Merville. Not far away there was a large, almost undamaged farm, with a spacious court-yard behind it. We looked rather longingly at this before setting up headquarters in the two cottages, but finally decided that comfort must be sacrificed for efficiency.

We did not regret the decision. A few hours later a

German self-propelled gun opened fire on the farmhouse and demolished it. Apart from this incident the rest of the night passed quietly enough. Nevertheless, all of us were tense and alert in our slit trenches. Sleep would have been impossible, even if it had been safe enough to try, for it was impossible to rest in the bottom of a narrow, muddy 'slitter.'

In this manner our first twenty-four hours in Normandy came to a close. Already our casualties were formidable for so comparatively small a force, being three officers and seventeen men killed and wounded, and one officer and twenty-eight men missing.

The officers killed and wounded were Bill Kennedy, our Intelligence Officer, who had been killed almost as soon as he stepped ashore on to Queen Red Beach; Lieutenant-Colonel N. C. Ries, our Commanding Officer; and Lieutenant Peter Nelson, Signals Officer, who had been wounded shortly after the C.O.

The missing officer was Lieutenant Peter Winston. No one knew what had happened to him. Together with his batman he had jumped with the Sixth Airborne Division on D Minus One, acting as Liaison Officer for our Brigade. He was to have met us on the Orne bridges at midday; but since he had departed from the unit about three weeks before D Day to join the Airborne Division at Salisbury we had not seen or heard of him.

And to-day, June 6, had been his 20th birthday, too.

CHAPTER 2

D PLUS ONE—June 7, 1944

AFTER the rather heavy casualties of the previous day (the Commando had been only about 450 strong in the first place) the only officers left in headquarters were Major Gray, Bryan White, and Hugh Smith, the Doctor.

Elsewhere in the Brigade things had not been going too well, either. We learned that 3 and 6 Commandos had had a desperate battle in and around Le Plein. The Germans had repeatedly counter-attacked, and had only been beaten off after heavy fighting.

At three o'clock in the morning Lord Lovat sent a signal to the effect that we were to withdraw from Merville at first light into the Brigade defensive positions now being hurriedly established at Le Plein, which lay three miles to the south.

Just over an hour later the unit prepared to move again. In the dim half-light of early morning men rose silently from their trenches to assemble on the line of march, silently buckling on their equipment, and reflectively rubbing the blackened stubble on their chins as they waited for the order to march.

Ten minutes later the advance to Le Plein commenced.

As the tail of our column was leaving Merville, enemy patrols were seen to enter the village from the far end.

However, our job was to rejoin the Brigade as soon as possible, not waste time engaging a party of the enemy who would needlessly hinder the operation and perhaps cause unwelcome casualties into the bargain, so we ignored them. Fortunately, they did not appear to see us. Even if they did, they were certainly reluctant to fight.

We reached Salanelles. It proved to be deserted—that is, it *looked* deserted. Nevertheless, we could not afford to take chances. The Commando fanned out into two columns, each moving down one side of the main street, from door to door, house to house, systematically clearing each one, making quite sure there were no enemy machine-gun or sniper posts lurking in the half-light.

Able Troop led the way through the village. Looking very warlike, Jock Rushforth, their Commander, poked his head out of the top window of a house half-way down the street, his hands on his rifle.

" *Come on,*" he yelled. " *I've got you covered!* "

This was to us. From his viewpoint Jock commanded the entire street, and could see whether or not there was any enemy in the vicinity. At the very same instant as he spoke, however, a very aged French madame, her hair still in curlers, poked her head out of the next-door window, saw Jock, then murmured resignedly, "*Mon Dieu, ces Anglais,*" and promptly disappeared.

Quite undaunted, Jock continued to lead the advance, and we reached Le Plein without further incident, apart from muttered cursing by Charlie Troop, who struggled manfully with their cycles up and down the immense craters with which our route was generously bestrewn—supplied by the R.A.F., of course.

Once in Le Plein we started to prepare our defensive positions in the area allotted to us by the Brigadier—an orchard to the left of the remainder of the Brigade's positions. By this time many of us had lost our picks and shovels, but these were readily supplied for the task by the local inhabitants, all of whom wanted to see us 'underground' as quickly as possible.

Shortly after our arrival some of the stragglers who had been left behind when Major Gray's party had been 'pinned down' on the outskirts of Salanelles the day before, came in. They looked tired, haggard, and dirty. Apparently they had made constant attempts to rejoin the Commando during the last twenty-four hours, but every time they moved they had been shot at by the ever-watchful enemy in the pill-box. Throughout the night they had carried out a miniature war of their own, killing at least two of the enemy in the process. One of our reconnaissance patrols, sent out to look for them, had eventually managed to extricate them.

During the course of the morning, Major Gray was called to Brigade headquarters for further orders. Whilst he was away the unit came under very accurate mortar fire from the direction of Salanelles. Bill Neaves replied with our own 'three-inchers' but was soon spotted by the enemy, who bombarded his positions so accurately that they sustained a direct hit and two casualties. As a result Bill and his Troop were obliged to make a rapid move to an alternative area.

Just as digging-in was more or less completed, our Jeeps —preloaded in England before the landing—began to arrive. They certainly proved a godsend. Much-needed ammunition, signal stores and medical supplies were hurriedly unloaded and distributed. The Jeep drivers then took on all the casualties they possibly could and ferried them at top speed to the beaches.

No sooner had these supplies arrived than a warning order came from Brigade headquarters that we were to stand by to advance once more—to where no one quite knew. We buckled on our equipment and awaited further orders.

A few minutes later Major Gray arrived back from his conference with the Brigadier, bringing with him a particularly heavy shower of mortar bombs which the enemy had deemed fit and proper to despatch at this juncture from the direction of Salanelles.

Major Gray called for an Orders Group to be assembled, and within a matter of minutes all the Unit Troop Commanders, together with Lieutenant-Colonel Peter Young (the C.O. of 3 Commando), two Troop Commanders from 3 Commando whose men were being placed under command of 45 Commando for this next operation, and two Forward Officers Bombardment (spotting for the Navy) were gathered round him to hear his orders.

We were going to attack Franceville-Plage.

3

In detail the plan was as follows. Forty-Five Commando was to advance to Franceville-Plage, whilst the two Troops from 3 Commando placed under command were to mop up the gun battery at Merville, destroying the one remaining gun which had apparently been shelling the beach area in a very annoying fashion. We were also to be given one 6-pounder anti-tank gun and some medium machine-guns to support us.

Half-way through Major Gray's orders the whole party was forced to take to the nearest ditch, owing to the fact that the mortars from Salanelles had started their tricks again. Major Gray continued to give his orders in between showers of bombs.

The enemy's bombardment of Le Plein still continued unabated as we moved off to the attack. The shelling and mortaring became very accurate, especially when we were moving through Salanelles.

Going down the main street of this village for the second time that day we suddenly heard the heartening noise of our medium machine-guns opening up on the enemy. This fire undoubtedly succeeded in making the Germans keep their heads down, enabling us to get through the village with comparatively few casualties.

Although the mortaring and shelling slackened a little it showed no signs of ceasing, and our casualties were steadily mounting in numbers. Bill Neaves lost two of his men— both of whom were carrying precious mortar barrels—as a result of the shelling, whilst one of our Jeeps, which had returned from the beach-head and was ferrying up ammunition for us, received a direct hit and exploded.

The loss of two mortars and a large quantity of ammunition—not to speak of the men—was later to prove a serious handicap. We sent a signal back to Brigade headquarters asking for replacements. Meanwhile the advance continued.

4

At about four o'clock that afternoon we came under heavy fire from the Merville Battery. Leaving one Troop behind to keep the latter busy, Major Gray took the rest of

c

us into Merville itself, where little or no resistance was encountered from the enemy.

The final orders for the attack on Franceville-Plage were given here, and whilst we were busy forming up, our objective was heavily bombarded by two cruisers and a destroyer of the Royal Navy, which were lying off the mouth of the Orne.

At precisely five minutes past five the attack started. The distance between Merville and the forward German positions at Franceville-Plage was about five hundred yards, across a stretch of flat, open country.

Advancing simultaneously Charlie and Easy Troops headed for the edge of the town, with Able Troop in rear to give them covering fire. Both the leading Troops covered this first ' bound ' without attracting any unwelcome attention from the enemy. They had undoubtedly seen us, but were waiting for us to get closer before opening up.

Some two hundred yards from the outskirts of Franceville-Plage Charlie Troop swung left to clear a wood lying to the east, almost at the mouth of the Orne. This proved to be full of enemy slit trenches, dug-outs and general defence works. Most of them were unoccupied, however, and those Germans who were in residence were quickly disposed of with the use of grenades. The Troop then took up a position on the left flank of the axis of advance, in order to provide protection to the main assaulting party, and at the same time to contain a strong German position at the very mouth of the Orne which had been temporaily ignored.

Major Gray's headquarter party, together with Able and Dog Troops, now moved forward to the edge of the wood which Charlie Troop had cleared, whilst Baker and Easy Troops moved into Franceville-Plage proper and

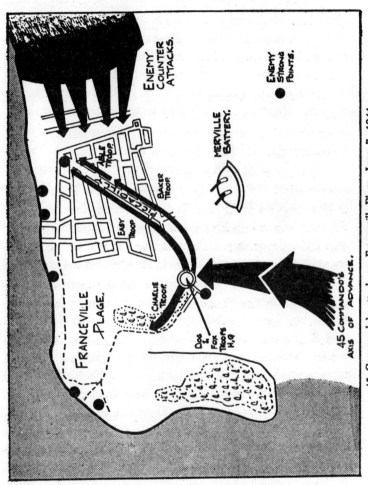

45 Commando's attack on Franceville-Plage, June 7, 1944

started to clear the main street—nicknamed 'Piccadilly' during the briefing for the operation. Baker Troop advanced down the left-hand side of 'Piccadilly' and Easy Troop down the right.

Whilst the Commando was carrying out this first deployment one of the Forward Officers Bombardment shinned up a nearby tree (where the Germans had thoughtfully built a very comfortable observation post) and continued to direct the fire of the Royal Navy to whom he was 'on call' by wireless.

During this period we could occasionally hear the sounds of battle behind us, which indicated that the two Troops of 3 Commando were now in action against the Merville Battery. Meanwhile our own attack proceeded.

A strong German pill-box dominated the whole of 'Piccadilly,' and was situated at the far end of the street. The two Troops continued their advance towards it, with Able Troop now following some distance behind Baker, to give assistance when and if required. Some distance from the pill-box both the leading Troops suddenly halted and went to ground. Accompanied by a PIAT party, consisting of himself and three men, Major Ian Beadle went forward to put a few bombs into this formidable-looking enemy position before launching a full-scale attack.

No sooner had the PIAT party showed themselves, however, than the enemy opened fire with mortars and machine-guns. Out of the four men lying there behind semi-cover one was killed and another wounded. A minor battle commenced almost immediately, with everyone on both sides blazing away furiously at each other, whilst down at the mouth of the river the German strong-point also opened up.

Wondering what the cause of the delay was at the far end of ' Piccadilly,' Major Gray, who had been following up the two leading Troops with his headquarter party, decided to go forward to see what was happening. Before he had advanced fifty yards a German anti-tank gun, firing down the length of ' Piccadilly,' scored a direct hit on his headquarters personnel, killing the R.S.M. and a corporal. Major Gray nevertheless continued to go forward, and having been given details of the situation by the leading Troops, ordered them to hold on to their present positions, and not to advance any further forward for the time being.

Meanwhile Dog Troop had moved out of the wood (where a temporary Commando headquarters and Regimental Aid Post had been set up) to follow the line of Easy Troop's advance. Bill Neaves had also set up his mortars in the wood, to give support when needed.

Able Troop, who had been following Baker Troop down ' Piccadilly,' suddenly came under intense fire at this stage from a hitherto silent enemy strong-point on the right flank. They immediately fanned out into the houses flanking the street and ' leap-frogged ' from one house to the other, advancing without further opposition until they came up to some German dug-outs on the extreme edge of the beaches to the north of the town. These they engaged with fire, whilst another Troop was ordered up by Major Gray to try and outflank them. Nevertheless, the attack was beaten off by the enemy, who was fighting with extreme determination.

But Major Gray was resolved to hold on at all costs, despite the fact that we were fast running out of ammunition, and that communications with Brigade headquarters at Le Plein were negligible.

There was a valiant attempt by Private Arnold, of Number 10 (Inter-Allied) Commando, who was attached to us for Intelligence duties, and who spoke excellent German, to bluff the enemy as to our real strength at this stage of the battle.

Approaching them alone, and with a white flag, Arnold called on the enemy to surrender, because there were at least three British divisions behind us, and that it would be a ' waste of blood ' to fight on. The Germans, however, were not to be bluffed. Their unhesitating answer was a vicious burst of machine-gun fire, followed almost immediately by a strong counter-attack to our right flank and rear.

The enemy's object now became all too clear. They were trying to cut us off, pushing us on to their beach defences at the mouth of the Orne, where we would be at the mercy of their guns.

Major Gray immediately decided to fight his way out. Turning about we started to retreat down ' Piccadilly,' in order to avoid being surrounded by vastly superior forces. A running fight ensued down the whole length of the main street, the Germans making frantic efforts to cut us off by moving their main counter-attacking force down a parallel street to our left.

As the Commando moved out, Able Troop, already badly cut up after their abortive engagement with the enemy near the beaches some minutes previously, were hurriedly reorganised by their subalterns—Tommy Thomas and Piers Dunkerley—in order to try and cover the unit's retreat by holding the enemy with fire. Their Troop Commander, Jock Rushforth, having been wounded a little earlier on, had been personally evacuated by Hugh Smith, who carried him on his back to a place of safety.

In the face of intense fire Able Troop held grimly on as the remainder of us headed for Merville : but they did

not escape further casualties. Piers Dunkerley was badly
wounded a few minutes later, leaving Tommy Thomas the
only officer in charge of the Troop.

5

On our way out of ' Piccadilly ' we found a sandy knoll
which dominated the greater part of Franceville-Plage by
virtue of its height. Major Gray gave orders for us to dig
in here—an easy matter in the soft sand—and from this
point patrols were sent out to try and contact some of our
many stragglers and wounded.

It was now eleven o'clock at night, and darkness was
upon us. With our ammunition very low indeed, and with
the large number of casualties and missing men, Major Gray
decided to withdraw the remnants of the unit to Merville,
which would be held for the night pending further orders.

We moved in silence to a knocked-out enemy strong-
point in a wood not far from the now quiet Merville Battery
in order to regroup ourselves, and try to make some provi-
sion for evacuating our scattered wounded to a place of
safety. Once the whole unit had reached the wood two
Troops were immediately despatched to clear Merville, into
which it was suspected the Germans had succeeded in re-
infiltrating. Fortunately for us our visit to Merville was
a surprise, and the enemy hastily abandoned their positions
to flee the village, no doubt thinking that the attacking force
was far larger than it actually was.

The rest of us accordingly began the march back into
Merville. Owing to the desperate fight we had to get out
of Franceville-Plage we had been forced to leave several
killed and wounded behind, in what was now technically

enemy territory Two of our medical orderlies, Lance-Corporals Relf and Dunlop—both of the R.A.M.C.—refused to leave the wounded entrusted to their care to the mercy of the enemy, and volunteered to stay behind with them. Later we learned that they were both captured.

By midnight we were occupying a tight, all-round defensive position in Merville. The strength of the unit was now considerably reduced, and it was still not known what had happened to the two Troops of 3 Commando. There was no trace whatsoever of them in Merville, which was not altogether surprising, in view of the fact that the enemy were still very definitely in the vicinity, holding as they did a small part of the village.

As far as communications were concerned our sole contact with Brigade headquarters at Le Plein was through the Forward Officer's Bombardment's wireless set to an H.Q. ship lying off the Orne, which was supposed to be relaying all messages on for us. In actual fact, however, we did not know if our signals were getting through when sent in this fashion, and if they were, what the time lag was.

In view of this Major Gray decided to send a small patrol through the enemy lines to Le Plein. Easy Troop were called upon to supply the men, and a few minutes after midnight Corporal Deacon and two others set out on their hazardous journey. Their task, if they reached Le Plein without mishap, was to let Lord Lovat know what the position was, and, if possible, to make arrangements for obtaining further supplies of ammunition and food for the entire Commando.

The rest of the night passed quietly. There was a strange stillness after the sweat and fury of the day. Now and again the crackle of rifle and machine-gun fire in the distance broke the stillness, and we in our slit trenches gripped our weapons and strained our eyes and ears as we waited for the enemy's coming.

But the enemy did not come. Like us, they were too exhausted.

CHAPTER 3

D PLUS TWO—June 8, 1944

EARLY the following morning Corporal Deacon's patrol returned. They had managed to slip through the German posts without being spotted, bringing with them a relief signalman. Communication with Brigade headquarters was thus restored.

The half-light of early morning soon transformed itself into watery daylight, and the enemy began to probe our positions again. German snipers crawled into activity, mortars started ranging on us, and the first shells of the day harmlessly straddled the Brigade defence perimeter.

We were getting used to the shelling and mortaring. It was the snipers who were so annoying. They seemed to foresee every move our men made, pushing our casualty figures even higher.

At half-past eight Major Gray received fresh orders from Lord Lovat. Merville was to be held at all costs. Orders were accordingly issued to all our Troop Commanders to tighten up the defences as much as possible.

Major Gray's orders were complied with : but what was worrying each and every one of us now was the ammunition situation. Supplies throughout the unit were very low, and it was obvious that drastic reallocation of all types to the fighting Troops most in need was very necessary.

26

All ammunition was therefore pooled, Commando headquarters giving up most of theirs to Able, Baker, Charlie,
Dog and Easy Troops.

Within an hour of receiving our orders from Lord Lovat
the first enemy attack came in from the direction of the
Merville Battery, accompanied by very heavy mortaring.
Somehow it was beaten off. All our bullets were carefully
counted, and every shot fired was aimed to kill.

2

About midday a couple of German Renault ambulances
drove into Merville, and two German drivers, a Polish
medical orderly and an Italian soldier got out and gave themselves up to us.

To say that we were surprised at this development
would be an understatement, for to us it seemed nothing
less than a miracle. After the confused fighting at Franceville-Plage we had only managed to collect eight of our
wounded, all of whom were at present lying on stretchers
in the R.A.P., requiring far greater attention than Hugh
Smith and his staff could possibly give them, owing to the
lack of surgical equipment. It would have been impossible
to evacuate them by stretcher-bearers to Le Plein, owing to
the open nature of the ground and the considerable distance
between ourselves and Brigade headquarters.

Major Gray decided to try and evacuate them to Le
Plein in the newly acquired ambulances, hoping against
hope that the intervening German outposts would show
some respect for the Red Cross flag. It was essential that
the wounded should receive early treatment, and when the
question of possible capture was raised we could only trust
that they would at least be well treated by the enemy.

One of the men attached to the unit from Number 10 Commando—Lance-Corporal Saunders—volunteered to conduct the party through the German lines. He himself had been wounded in the leg, and spoke very good German. The four prisoners who had given themselves up to us seemed to be willing to co-operate.

The eight casualties and one very badly wounded German prisoner were therefore loaded into the two ambulances. This involved a stretcher carry across a much-sniped orchard from Hugh Smith's R.A.P., but was successfully accomplished under the protection of the Red Cross flag. The Germans, rather surprisingly, respected the flag when they saw it on this occasion, although this was not always to be the case, as we were to find later on in the campaign.

Led by Lance-Corporal Saunders the ambulances drove off, heading south for Le Plein: but only just in time, for the barn where the loading took place was set on fire five minutes later by extremely accurate and unpleasant shelling from an enemy anti-tank gun. This same gun also succeeded in hitting the R.A.P., whereupon Hugh Smith and his staff had to evacuate immediately.

Despite the efforts of Lance-Corporal Saunders, together with the frantic explanations of the German drivers, the two ambulances were recaptured by the enemy. Saunders managed to escape, and told us that all the casualties had been taken back by the Germans to their own dressing station for treatment. Later we learned that they were transferred to the German base hospital at Pont L'Eveque.

3

Whilst all this had been going on, the Forward Officer Bombardment had been in touch with a Fleet destroyer by wireless, requesting further support from naval guns on to the enemy positions in Franceville-Plage. As usual, the Navy obliged, supplying a series of earthquake-like salvoes which more than succeeded in keeping the Germans quiet. Needless to say, the incessant mortaring which we had endured for the greater part of the day now ceased.

For some extraordinary reason the enemy now decided to indulge in a little game amongst themselves. The Germans in the Merville Battery, probably thinking that British troops still remained in Franceville-Plage, started to mortar the southern edge of the town. In actual fact a small party of Germans were occupying these positions now, and consequently it was most amusing for us to watch the proceedings.

Nevertheless, there was little for us to laugh about really. Our ammunition state was, by this time, extremely critical, and as it was impossible to pool any more from Commando headquarters, Major Gray ordered out two patrols, with instructions to recover as much ammunition as possible from the rucksacks of the wounded which had been ' dumped ' before the attack on Franceville-Plage.

Fortunately for us the patrols achieved some measure of success. Enough small arms ammunition was obtained to keep the unit going for a little longer, until such time as Brigade headquarters could arrange to send up some more.

The time was now half-past twelve in the morning. We were too tightly surrounded by this time to allow any further patrols to try and slip out to procure more ammunition from the vicinity of Franceville-Plage, and half an hour later the enemy launched their second attack on us. It was a very determined one, and in considerable strength.

The German assault came in from two directions—the east, and the north. As in the first attack we carefully conserved our ammunition, shooting to kill at the closest possible range, so that no ammunition would be wasted. Eventually we succeeded in beating the enemy off once more.

One of the German infantrymen captured after this attack told us that only eighteen men out of his company had survived our withering defensive fire. The normal battle strength of a German infantry company was then reckoned at about 100-120 men, incidentally.

Major Gray had a narrow escape during this attack. Whilst going round the unit positions he turned the corner of a track leading out of Merville, only to find himself face to face with a couple of Germans, fumbling hurriedly with a Spandau machine-gun as they prepared what they obviously thought was going to prove a disconcerting ambush.

Both Major Gray and the enemy were surprised, to say the least : but fortunately reaction on our side was quicker. Whipping out his .45 Colt automatic Major Gray shot them both through the head.

This summary despatching of two of the ' bad men,' as Major Gray called them, served to increase the great admiration which everyone already had for him.

At one o'clock (lunch time, only there was no lunch) Lord Lovat sent us a further signal, to the effect that all attempts to relieve us had failed, and that we were to rejoin the Brigade as soon as possible after dark.

It is difficult to try and express our feelings, as they were then. For two days and nights we had been without sleep, and had had precious little food. Apart from that, our casualties were considerable, for we had lost a quarter of our total strength in killed, wounded and missing. More than anything else, we were trying to hold an area of ground

out of which the enemy would eventually throw us by virtue
of his numerical superiority.

We counted the hours to darkness. Nine or ten, at
least. No food till then. Would we be able to sleep when
we got to Le Plein? What about our ammunition if the
enemy attacked again?

Nine or ten hours. It seemed a long time. Distressingly
long.

4

Throughout the afternoon the Germans surrounding the
village gave us no respite whatsoever. They mortared our
positions and sniped us continually. Just before three
o'clock a small party of the enemy succeeded in working
their way into Merville from the east, bringing up extra
machine-gun teams and snipers. However, two sergeants
attached to us from 10 Commando—Sergeants Shelley and
Stewart—put a stop to this ruse. Unknown to the enemy,
they succeeded in crawling up to the side of a barn, on the
other side of which the newly arrived party of Germans
were hastily setting up a machine-gun post, and lobbed grenades over the roof. These fell right amongst them,
wounding two (who were captured) and putting the
remainder to flight.

Three hours later further enemy movement was
observed to the west of Merville. We prepared ourselves
for another full-scale attack. Then one of our men in a
forward position reported that the Germans appeared to be
trying to attract our attention, for they were shouting and
waving their arms about.

It was not really clear what the enemy were trying to
do. They might be trying to trick us into thinking that they

wanted to collect their wounded, then launch an assault
from the opposite direction. We had already learned that
it was never safe to trust them in this respect.

The Germans still continued to gesticulate. We did not
go forward, but merely ' stood to ' in our slit trenches,
waiting to see what they would do next.

It was just as well we did.

Within a matter of minutes the enemy had launched
the third big attack of the day against us—from the opposite
end of the village. At first sight it appeared to be a really
determined effort on the part of the attackers, who were
being supported by vicious-looking self-propelled guns which
rumbled ominously down the main street of Merville,
knocking down the flimsy French houses one by one as they
pumped shells into them.

Another attack, dwindling ammunition, and at least five
hours to go before we could withdraw to Le Plein. The
situation was not so good.

Major Gray decided that the time had come to get out
of Merville. Under the very noses of the enemy in the
nearby Battery the Commando was withdrawn through
thickly wooded country, sorting itself out hurriedly into
its various Troops on the move. ·

By night such a withdrawal would have been bad
enough. In broad daylight it was even worse. Once clear
of the village we pressed on with all speed for Le Plein.
Meanwhile, to our rear, we could hear the Germans hunting
around for us in a now deserted Merville, blazing away
furiously with everything they had. To cover our retreat
the Forward Officer Bombardment set up his box of tricks,
and soon the Navy out at sea were bringing down the most
effective fifteen-inch gunfire on the village.

As we marched on down that dusty road which was leading us with every step a few yards nearer to our comrades in First S.S. Brigade we all breathed a sigh of relief. At last we had escaped an enemy who had persistently harassed us ever since our enforced withdrawal from Franceville-Plage. Ahead of us lay the comparative shelter of the Brigade defence perimeter, food, ammunition, and perhaps, sleep. . . .

For the next half-mile nothing happened. Then, Easy Troop, who were leading the Commando, suddenly halted and went to ground. The rest of us automatically followed suit. A few minutes later a panting Marine from Easy Troop reported to Major Gray with a message from Ian Beadle. The leading Troop had been ' pinned down ' by four German machine-gun posts to their immediate front which had not yet been accurately located.

As Major Gray started to move forward to see the situation for himself a second runner reported from Ian Beadle. The posts had now been located, and it looked as if any attempt to outflank them would be doomed to failure from the start. On the right flank the ground was mined, whilst on the left there was not only the notorious Merville Battery, but also other enemy defences.

The only possible solution to overcome this problem was to assault the four machine-gun posts direct. They certainly could not be ignored. Major Gray ordered Easy Troop to hold the enemy by fire whilst he took a chance with the rest of the Commando, leading them round as quietly as possible on the left flank, along a line of hedges between two other known German positions.

Fortunately these latter positions did not bother us; and it was at this stage that Sergeant John Brown, and Marine Norman Green, both of Easy Troop, saved the situation.

D

Mustering as many 68-type grenades as he could from the men in his section, Sergeant Brown took up an exposed position so as to draw the enemy's fire, then engaged them with his grenades, firing them from his rifle by means of a discharger-cup. In this way he accounted for two of the German machine-gun posts.

Meanwhile Green, a Bren-gunner, calmly crawled out of the ditch in which he was laying to lie down in an open field, where he set up his Bren gun. He was seen almost immediately by the enemy, drawing the combined fire of the remaining machine-gun posts.

Quite undeterred, Green commenced to return their fire. Bren-gun magazines were filled and flung to him by his comrades, who were still lying hidden in the ditch fifteen yards away. Unfortunately one of the German machine-gunners succeeded in hitting, not Green, but the magazine on top of his gun, which in a matter of seconds became a blazing mass.

Green immediately wrenched the magazine off, picking up another which had been flung at him. Despite the fact that he stood a very good chance of being hit by the exploding magazine at his side, he nevertheless continued to engage the enemy. In this way he eventually disposed of the remaining German posts.

For this conspicuous bravery both Green and Sergeant Brown were later awarded the Military Medal.

5

We took only one prisoner as a result of this action, together with booty in the shape of two Spandau machine-guns, two 81-millimetre mortars, and a German motor-cycle.

All of us were beginning to feel very tired now. Our

shoulders were aching with the weight of rucksacks and
other equipment which we had been carrying for almost
three days, with very little rest.

We regained our original axis of advance, and prepared
to march those last two miles into Le Plein.

Moving through the fields and back gardens which lay
to the south of Salanelles, we passed through the tiny village
of Hauger, almost adjoining Le Plein, and eventually
reached Number 4 Commando's lines, having picked up a
few German stragglers en route, who were just as tired as
we were, and only too pleased to give themselves up.

Once in 4 Commando's area we knew that at last we
had safely reached the Brigade defence perimeter. We
rested our weary bodies in a sunken lane, and there met
Lieutenant-Colonel Peter Young, the C.O. of 3 Commando.

To our dismay he told us that we had arrived back in
Le Plein right in the middle of a particularly heavy battle,
and that the Brigade had been heavily attacked throughout
the day.

However, his news was not all quite so discouraging to
our now almost exhausted unit. Although our attack on
Franceville-Plage had proved abortive, by holding Merville
for the length of time we did, we had successfully contained
all the German units to the north of Le Plein, thus splitting
their main attacking force in half. In addition to this, our
unexpected arrival in Le Plein, where we had not been
expected until late that night, had considerably heartened
the remainder of the Brigade.

Major Gray received orders from Lord Lovat at this
stage that we were to rest immediately. We made our way
to the tiny little church standing in the centre of the village
green, and there bedded down for what we hoped was going
to be a long night's sleep. Within minutes we were dead

to the world, blissfully unaware of the battle raging round us on the outskirts of Le Plein—a battle that was being fought by Numbers 3, 4 and 6 Commandos against an enemy who were apparently as relentless as those who had so mercilessly harassed us at Merville throughout the day and the previous night.

Aching limbs and sore backs were forgotten as we slept that long night's sleep in the shadow of the High Altar. Brigade headquarters, realising how tired we were, provided the necessary guards to watch over us, and to call us out again should Lord Lovat need us for battle before the dawn.

But we weren't needed, thank God.

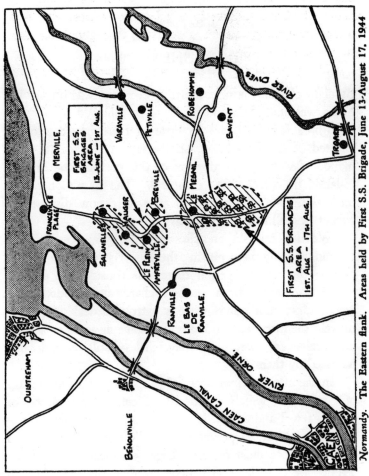

Normandy. The Eastern flank. Areas held by First S.S. Brigade, June 13–August 17, 1944

CHAPTER 4

PERIOD JUNE 9-12, 1944

By eight o'clock the next morning everyone was up, having had a welcome wash and shave, to be followed by our first good breakfast for days. A little later we moved into our allotted defensive position, on the left of Number 6 Commando. With our occupation of this position the Brigade ' island ' of defence was complete. The four Commando units comprising First S.S. Brigade were now disposed in a tight ring all round the village.

We dug our slit trenches as quickly as possible, and by mid-morning were putting the finishing touches to them. During the digging period there was considerable activity by German snipers from nearby orchards and wooded areas. Major Gray sent out numerous patrols to deal with these unwelcome intruders, and although some measure of success was achieved, we were nevertheless still considerably harassed by them.

In the afternoon we sent fighting patrols into the village of Amfreville, which adjoined Le Plein, being a matter of only a few hundred yards to the east. Here enemy were encountered but, surprisingly, they did not put up much of a fight. Once most of the village was clear, Ian Beadle's Troop were ordered to take over a disused German N.A.A.F.I.—vacated by the enemy for reasons best known to themselves some days before—and to maintain a standard sniping party to deal with anyone who attempted to re-infiltrate into Le Plein.

Meanwhile, further houses were cleared of odd Germans by other unit patrols in various parts of Amfreville. These German troops must have known that they were cut off, but did not give in without first showing fight. There was a lot of close-quarters work between our men and the trapped Germans at this stage, but our bag of prisoners was steadily mounting. One of the prisoners we pulled in was a somewhat suspicious-looking little gentleman who claimed that he was a Spanish Socialist and had been forced to work for the Germans. We sent him back to the Brigade Intelligence Officer, and never heard of him again.

2

The day was the quietest we had enjoyed since landing in Normandy. It was obvious now that the enemy were as tired and short of supplies as we were: but again, like us, they were busily re-grouping. Even though they launched no full-scale attacks on us, they nevertheless continued to harass us with snipers and patrols, which tried to penetrate the Brigade defence ring from all points of the compass.

Early the following morning, June 10, a fighting patrol from Easy Troop under Ian Beadle was sent into the neigh-bouring village of Breville, which lay to the east again of Amfreville.

This village was known to be held in strength by the enemy, believed to be part of an S.S. formation. The object of Ian Beadle's patrol was to ascertain the approximate strength of the German force, and to obtain some idea of its defensive lay-out.

The patrol set off at half-past four in the morning, whilst it was still dark. They succeeded in penetrating Breville and, despite the blind, confused shooting by both sides which followed, inflicted many casualties on German outposts. The actual battle strength of the German force in Breville could not be assessed with any degree of accuracy, however.

Ian Beadle returned with his men some two hours later, at half-past six, and nothing further happened until eight o'clock. Then the first enemy attack of the day came in. It was pushed hard, swiftly, and with great determination. One prong thrust at 6 Commando on our left, swinging round across the wooded country which lay to our front. This, in the words of Major Gray, provided the unit with some very satisfactory shooting, for we caught the enemy in enfilade.

The attack continued for the next four hours: but by midday it began to shows signs of weakening. Throughout the morning wave after wave of German infantry had flung themselves against 6 Commando and ourselves, supported by heavy mortar and machine-gun fire. Each time we had, with difficulty, beaten them off.

Despite this gradual abatement of the fury of the attack, however, there still appeared to be several strong pockets of resistance in the woods to our front, and Major Gray decided to eliminate these while the going was good.

At twenty minutes past one, a fighting patrol, fifty strong, was sent out into the woods, with the task of clearing them as extensively as possible. The patrol returned at three o'clock, to report that a considerable area had been cleared, and numerous casualties inflicted upon the enemy. They also told us that another wood, half a mile beyond, was affording excellent cover to German half-tracked vehicles which appeared to be moving into position there.

Major Gray wasted no time. He immediately ordered
Bill Neaves into action with his three-inch mortars. A
heavy concentration of bombs was put down by the latter's
mortar teams on the wood, during which time a second
patrol moved out to investigate the results.

Our mortaring of the woods was highly successful.
The patrol returned some two hours later, with the information that they had reached the wood, where no live Germans
were seen, but that there had been a lot of dead lying
around, and one German half-track vehicle put out of
action.

Shortly before six o'clock Bill Neaves' mortars went into
action again—this time against a small party of the enemy
who had re-infiltrated into Amfreville unobserved. The
mortars completely disorganised them, and the survivors
retreated in no uncertain manner. Whether this had been
the prelude to another attack we never knew; but at any
rate this was the last interference on the enemy's part that
day.

Throughout the night we ' stood to ' in our slit trenches
in shifts, waiting for an enemy who never came. It was
often like that. We became so bored and sleepy with waiting that we would have almost welcomed an attack.

Midnight came, and still the enemy remained silent.
There was no mortaring, no shelling, no suspicious movement. The hours of early morning ticked slowly by. One
o'clock . . . two o'clock . . . three . . . four in the morning,
and nothing had happened. It was all very suspicious. Of
course, the enemy might be enjoying a good night's rest.
But could they be doing this whilst we were here, waiting
for them?

It seemed very much as if this was the case. As the
twinkling of the stars slowly subdued to the first clear

streaks of early dawn, officers and N.C.O.s went their
rounds, and everywhere reports were the same—all quiet.

And then, at about four-thirty, it began.

3

For over twenty minutes we received one of the heaviest
mortarings we had yet experienced. A little after five
o'clock, Easy Troop, who were still in their ex-German
N.A.A.F.I. in Amfreville, reported that they were being
attacked by infantry and self-propelled guns. Fortunately
the latter were shelling Easy Troop with but little effect.

The battle raged at spasmodic intervals throughout the
whole day. Quite early on, and for some reason best known
to themselves, the enemy made no attempt to push their
attack home, being content to harass us with very heavy
mortaring and machine-gun fire.

At about half-past ten that night a battalion of the
Black Watch from the 51st (Highland) Division formed up
on the village green of Amfreville. We were told that they
were going to attack Breville. Twenty minutes later their
assault began, only to be met with most determined enemy
opposition.

Major Gray was now ordered by Brigade headquarters
to provide another fighting patrol to assist the Black Watch.
The patrol moved off at half-past eleven, and again succeeded in penetrating the German defences at Breville—
as they had done that morning—much to the surprise of
the Scottish troops. . . .

Once inside Breville we had another deadly shooting
match in the dark with the Germans. Our casualties this
time were three wounded, all of whom were successfully
evacuated to Amfreville by our own stretcher-bearers. The

enemy's casualties, on the other hand, would certainly seem to have been more than ours, but we could not estimate them.

Soon after the return of our fighting patrol a special party, four strong, and under the command of Lieutenant John Day, was sent into the enemy-held part of Amfreville to see what they could find. They were fortunate in securing a prisoner, who at last gave us a definite clue as to the identity of the German formation we were up against in the Breville area.

We might have guessed who these Germans were in the first place. The scared, captured soldier was identified as an S.S. trooper, belonging to the Reconnaisance Regiment of the notorious 21st Panzer Division.

John Day's party also found two 81-millimetre mortars, their trailers full of bombs, and two enemy half-track vehicles, on each of which was mounted a 2-centimetre flak gun. When Brigade headquarters learned of this they immediately despatched a strong patrol from 6 Commando to bring the booty in.

4

For the last two days everything had been very quiet: and it was to be the same on the following day, June 12 —at least until night fell.

Throughout the whole of the morning, and the greater part of the afternoon, nothing happened beyond the usual shelling and mortaring. A reconnaissance patrol of men from Easy Troop set out at eight o'clock in the morning, to report upon return that they had seen only one German in the enemy-held area of Amfreville.

It seemed as if the enemy were now concentrating their main force in the stronghold of Breville. They were obviously determined to make a stand there, whatever happened, knowing that if they lost the village they would have to fall back on the wooded areas to the east, which formed a vast, natural screen, sufficient to conceal an entire army.

But if they had been forced to completely withdraw their troops from Amfreville they had nevertheless succeeded in holding a considerable portion of the ground to the north, retaining control of Franceville-Plage, which dominated the mouth of the Orne and the now devastated town of Ouistreham. On the other hand, however, First S.S. Brigade had established itself in good defensive positions around Le Plein and Amfreville, with Sixth Airborne Division on their right, and 4th S.S. Brigade on their left, occupying a line running almost due north from the tiny village of Hauger to the sea. 4th S.S. Brigade, incidentally, had had a variety of special jobs to do since D Day. Whereas our Brigade had been working as a single formation, 4th S.S. Brigade—consisting of Numbers 41, 46, 47 and 48 Royal Marine Commandos—had each carried out individual tasks on landing, linking up as a Brigade on D plus two.

Both the Sixth Airborne Division and 4th S.S. Brigade had had proportionately as many casualties as ourselves. In fact the whole of this left flank of the Anglo-American bridgehead was being held—although we certainly did not know it then—more by sheer bluff than by anything else. Many of the units here had nearly as many German Spandaus as they had British Bren guns, so depleted were they in equipment, not to speak of men.

From ten o'clock onwards that morning our unit was standing by to provide a special patrol (if needed) to assist in the next assault on Breville which, we understood, was now going to be attempted by the 12th Parachute Battalion, not the Black Watch.

The task which our patrol had been given was the clearing of a large house on the outskirts of Breville, known to be occupied in strength by the enemy, and which might interfere with the main attack on the village proper.

The 12th Parachute Battalion did not begin their assault until ten o'clock that night. In the meantime heavy Sherman tanks had rumbled into position on the village green at Amfreville to support them, whilst behind us, five miles away, whole field regiments of the Royal Artillery were preparing the way for the paratroops by ' softening up ' the German positions in Breville with very heavy shelling. This, coupled with the blazing counter-fire which the Germans put down on Le Plein when they heard the Shermans moving into position, created something of an inferno.

Everyone seemed to be shouting to try and make their orders heard above the roar of gunfire. The men of our patrol, with their usual blackened faces, stood silhouetted in the flash of explosions as they advanced down the road running into Breville—an almost suicidal thing to do, for the Germans were raking the road with Spandau fire; but the advance went on.

Meanwhile, under cover of billowing clouds of smoke and dust, the parachute battalion followed us in for the main assault.

6

It was a very costly battle, raging throughout the night. Eventually Breville was taken, but not without considerable casualties to ourselves. It was estimated that something like 160 stretcher cases were evacuated through our positions alone that night—most of them paratroopers. Our own patrol did not come out entirely unscathed, either, for out of the one and twenty who set out, only ten returned. Four men were killed, and seven others wounded.

CHAPTER 5

PERIOD JUNE 13-AUGUST 16, 1944

AFTER six days of hard fighting both sides now began to settle down to a long period of static warfare. The Germans were in quite as reduced a state as we were, and whilst the orders of Sixth Airborne Division—with the two Special Service Brigades under command—were simply to contain the enemy on the left flank of the Allied beach-head, dominating the sector by aggressive patrolling, there was no doubt that the enemy, for their part, were quite incapable of mounting any further attacks in strength on our front.

Before commencing patrolling on a large scale we had to sort ourselves out. In the first place the entire Brigade had suffered many casualties, including the Brigade Commander, Lord Lovat, who had been severely wounded by shellfire during the first few days, and had to be evacuated to England for treatment. His place as Brigadier was taken by the senior Commando C.O. in the Brigade, Lieutenant-Colonel Derek Mills-Roberts. A Guards Territorial officer, Colonel Mills-Roberts was a veteran of the North African campaign. Command of his unit—Number 6 Commando—was now given to Major 'Tony' Lewis, of the Dorset Regiment.

We did not know it then, but this was to prove the beginning of the build-up of a magnificent fighting machine,

for our new Brigadier was the man who was going to weld
us. A small, slight man in his middle thirties, his hair almost
completely white, he had been a solicitor in private life. He
had immense drive, and a whiplash personality. It was he,
and he alone, who made the First Commando Brigade—as
it was ultimately named—one of the finest independent
formations in the North-West European theatre, and which
as such, ultimately earned the personal thanks of the Commander of British Second Army, Lieutenant-General Sir
Miles Dempsey.

Then there were the Colonels. 3 Commando was commanded by Lieutenant-Colonel Peter Young, who joined
the Commandos in their very early days. He was a very
young C.O., with a puckish sense of humour, a man who
had been ' in ' at Dieppe and sundry other raids before ever
coming to Normandy.

4 Commando was led by Lieutenant-Colonel Dawson.
They were a unit who had earned a considerable reputation
as fighting troops before D Day, and Dawson, a quiet, like-
able man, was carrying on the great tradition which Lord
Lovat, as the original C.O. of the Commando, had created.

Mills-Roberts' old Commando—Number 6—had, needless to say, already been welded into a unit with a terrific
fighting spirit. They, too, were veterans of North Africa,
having served under command of British First Army, and
' Tony ' Lewis, their new C.O., slim, fair-haired, twenty-six
year old, already had their confidence.

Lastly there was ourselves, Number 45 Royal Marine
Commando, commanded by Major (now Lieutenant-
Colonel) Nicol Gray. We were the only unit in the Brigade
which had never been in action before D Day.

Nicol Gray was a 36-year-old bachelor, standing six
foot two in his socks, and as strong as an ox. His face was

an interesting one. He had cold, blue eyes which instantly commanded respect; a massive, shaggy skull, with a high, clear-thinking forehead; and a thin, compressed mouth which, together with his broad, firm chin, indicated unerring determination.

He had only commanded us for a few days: but already he held our universal confidence. His coolness whilst directing the withdrawal during the battle of Franceville-Plage had won our silent admiration. He was a great leader.

2

We now tried to reorganise ourselves as far as possible. As far as our unit was concerned, there were one or two minor changes amongst the officers—mainly due to casualties amongst our Troop Commanders—which had to be effected first. Bryan White, our Adjutant, went to command Able Troop, replacing Jock Rushforth, who had been wounded and evacuated. His place at Commando headquarters was taken by Bill Neaves, command of the mortar and machine-gun teams in the Heavy Weapons Troop being taken by Lieutenant Colin Fletcher.

Apart from these changes, weapons, stores and transport were replaced within the unit as far as possible; but most important of all, we started to get regular sleep, meals, and baths. We even kept ourselves fit, too, by carrying out P.T. on the village green whenever we could.

We never relaxed our efforts to perfect and strengthen our defensive positions. After the Breville battle the Germans had completely vacated that village, so that now we had Brigade headquarters, 3, 6 and 45 Commandos defending the adjoining villages of Le Plein and Amfreville, whilst

E

4 Commando moved to take over the badly shelled, almost uninhabitable collection of houses and cottages that was Breville.

The enemy, for their part, had fallen back meanwhile on excellent defensive positions lying on the forward edge of the wooded area about a mile to the east. From our preliminary patrolling activities we had learned that they were putting down a quantity of mines and barbed wire around their positions. It definitely appeared that they were there to stay.

Nevertheless, the Germans did not like these patrols of ours, which were carried out almost invariably at night. Supported by tremendous artillery, mortar, and machine-gun fire, they had a bad effect on their morale. From our point of view, however, they were invaluable, for thanks to them we never lost confidence or that essential spirit of aggression through inactivity.

A typical patrol carried out by us was 'Operation Viper,' which took place on the night of June 27-28.

3

Brigadier Mills-Roberts had ordered our Commando to carry out a large-scale fighting patrol action against the enemy on a small front in the wooded area some fifteen hundred yards to the east of Amfreville.

Able Troop were selected by Colonel Gray for the job, with Lieutenant Tommy Thomas, a South African who had fought in Abyssinia and the Libyan desert, in command.

For this operation Able Troop were to have immense support fire, consisting of Artillery 25-pounders, Vickers medium machine-guns, and all the three-inch mortars available in our Brigade. The fire plan was for the Gunners to put down a tremendous ' softening ' concentration of shells in the area of the woods to be assaulted by our men. This would be lifted as soon as the attack on the enemy positions started. Meanwhile the medium machine-guns and mortars were to ' blanket-off ' the area by firing down on either side of the assault lane.

The entire raid would be controlled by Colonel Gray who, with a party of Gunners—acting as spotters for the Artillery—and a small protection group, would take up a position some three hundred yards from the German lines.

We moved off from Amfreville at eight o'clock on the night of June 27, Able Troop leading. Everyone wore berets and gym shoes, carrying weapons ranging from fighting knives and rifles to PIATs and K guns.*

We had to move very quietly, for the only route out to No Man's Land which was not mined was along a metalled road. We passed through Number 3 Commando's lines, the usual long, silent snake of men. There was a temporary pause whilst password and countersign were exchanged with a lone Commando sentry, then we were beyond the Brigade defence perimeter.

We still had a long way to go, but everyone grew more wary now, quietly fumbling with the mechanism of rifles or tommy-guns to make quite sure they were cocked. The distance between us and 3 Commando may still have been only a matter of yards, but we couldn't afford to take chances, nevertheless. German patrols into our lines in the past had proved more than cunning. One never knew whether or not a wandering party of the enemy had spotted us, and all unknown, was laying an ambush.

---

* A specially adapted light machine-gun used by Commando troops, fitted with 100-round magazines, and capable of a high rate of fire

Overhead, the moon was clear and cool, and the stars shone like tiny, elegant jewels in the cloak of night. The air was fresh and invigorating. It did not seem possible that somewhere in front of us crouched a miserable collection of German infantry in muddy pits, straining their eyes in the darkness as they waited for an attack.

The road from Amfreville ran due east, straight towards the enemy. Within half an hour of starting out we had covered twelve hundred yards, and at this stage Colonel Gray and his party left the main column to take up a posi-tion off the road, in the corner of a small wood, to set up their wireless and wait until Able Troop had formed up ahead for the main assault.

The night was deathly quiet, broken only by the distant, occasional rumble of guns somewhere in the north-west of Caen, away on our right.

Colonel Gray's party quickly took up their position, whilst the Gunners set up their wireless, as did our own Commando personnel, maintaining contact with Brigade at Amfreville. The protection group formed a close defensive ring all round, covering every possible avenue of approach.

The area stank of dead bodies. Most of the protection group appeared to be lying near German corpses which had been there for some days, even since the first few hours of hectic fighting, when the Sixth Airborne Division dropped out of the skies.

Suddenly, the quietness of the night was broken by the eerie crackle of wireless. Operators were calling up their parent formations.

" Hallo, Dog Easy Fox. Report my signals. I say again, report my signals. Dog Easy Fox . . . over."

The crackling became louder, more insistent, as the

operator at the other end replied, his voice seeming to come from nowhere in the darkness.

"*Hallo, Dog Easy Fox. Am hearing you strength five . . . strength five . . . Dog Easy Fox . . . over.*"

We all began to glance anxiously at our watches now. The luminous dials showed the time to be two minutes to ten.

Two minutes to go. Then the artillery would open up. Thirty seconds later Able Troop reported to Colonel Gray by wireless that they were in position.

That was all we wanted to know.

Punctually at ten o'clock the air was filled with a dull, rumbling noise which started from some distance to our rear. Within seconds dozens of shells were whistling overhead, to smack a little later with sickening precision on the enemy positions. To add to the steady coughing of the guns was joined the high-pitched chatter of Vickers medium machine-guns, and the steady popping sound of three-inch mortars, whose bombs exploded at half-minute intervals with a lingering whine.

For the next thirty minutes the noise was incessant. All of us with Colonel Gray's party lay perfectly still as that deadly blanket of high explosive passed overhead; and every now and then, faintly above the roar of gunfire, could be heard the steady, monotonous voices of wireless operators lying near us, sending back a constant stream of range corrections over the air to the Gunners.

At half-past ten Tommy Thomas sent a message to us over his wireless saying that he was ready to move into the final assault. For the ten minutes following his terse announcement we heard nothing. Then, suddenly, the enemy-held woods three hundred yards to our front began

to fill with the crackle of rifle and tommy-gun fire, coupled
with the sharp burst of grenades and the spasmodic, withering noise of a K gun as it opened fire to silence a position.

Able Troop were in amongst the Germans.

4

We could do nothing now but wait for Tommy
Thomas's next signal—that he had successfully withdrawn
all his men. Then we could open up with artillery and
mortars again to cover his retreat.

We lay there for an hour and a half before we heard
from Tommy again, during which time we had become
worried, to say the least, for we thought that the worst
had happened. At three minutes to midnight, however, we
received a reassuring message from Tommy to the effect
that he and his Troop were proceeding home independently.
Colonel Gray immediately informed the Gunners, and
within a matter of seconds the inferno had started again,
artillery, mortars and Vickers all laying down fire according
to their prearranged programme.

It was time for us to get out, too. We rose rapidly to
our feet, and hastily formed up in single file on the road
leading back to Amfreville. Meanwhile the obliging Gunners kept up their fire for another ten minutes or so, then
all became quiet again, as it had been three hours before.

Once in Amfreville we made for our agreed rendezvous
—Chateau Nixon, Lieutenant-Colonel Peter Young's headquarters, named after the Commando officer who had captured it. Here we met Tommy Thomas, his white teeth
creasing his blackened face into an enormous grin. He told
us that the raid had been highly successful, and that our
casualties had been only two in number, both of them slight.

Apparently Able Troop had managed to get right behind
the enemy lines, and had been allowed to do pretty well
what they pleased by the frightened Germans, who seemed
thoroughly demoralised after their intense shelling. Consequently a lot of them had been eliminated by the men of
Able Troop, and Tommy himself had had quite a glorious
time wandering around the enemy's area, tossing grenades
into farm buildings which he suspected to be headquarters
or storehouses.

Leading Able Troop back through the enemy lines again
towards Amfreville had not been anything like so easy. The
Germans had rallied themselves, putting up a desperate fight
to try and trap the raiders by surrounding them and cutting
off their line of escape. Able Troop, however, had fought
their way out, and that, said Tommy, was all there was to it.

But such was not entirely the case. The South African
did not tell us that he had been wounded in the leg very
early on during the attack, and had refused either to leave
his men or abandon the operation because of it. For this
fine piece of leadership and personal bravery he later
received the Military Cross.

5

Such raids as these gave us complete moral superiority
over the Germans on the left flank. We inflicted numerous
casualties upon them at relatively small cost to ourselves—
so much so that, from the beginning of July onwards, we
never had a single raid on our positions, either by night or
day. Our dominancy of No Man's Land was, in fact, complete.

By day we used to send out small sniping parties, pro-
tected by standing patrols of anything up to one Troop in

strength. These sniping expeditions were generally successful, as they deserved to be, for it was extremely hazardous
to venture as close to the enemy's positions in broad daylight
as our snipers did, crawling to within a distance of one
hundred yards. There they would lie in wait, heavily camou-
flaged, in a nearby hedgerow: motionless, despite the fact
that they were, as often as not, plagued incessantly by
mosquitoes.

One of the best snipers in our Commando was a Marine
named Cakebread. A hairdresser before the war, Cakebread accounted for over thirty Germans in the Normandy
campaign alone.

Towards the end of July it became necessary to dis-
continue our raids as the enemy had found an effective
counter to them in the shape of mines and booby-traps, with
which they had surrounded their positions in the most
generous manner. In any case, we had received orders to
move from our present area around Le Plein and Amfreville
so that we could take over a new sector of the line from an
Airborne unit. There was, apparently, to be a general re-
shuffling of Airborne and Commando units on the left flank
at this stage. The object of this was to deceive the enemy
as to the exact identity of the troops opposite them, and also
to relieve our own men in the more nerve-racking parts of
the line, giving them a " rest " elsewhere.

By now the importance of this flank we were holding
had become apparent. British Second Army suddenly
launched a break-out to the south-east of Caen, with heavy
support from tanks and aircraft. This proved abortive—
mainly, we were told, to the bad weather, which had bogged
down the tanks in mud and severely hampered air operations. For us, however, the realisation that the left flank
had to be held at all costs became more and more clear. Our

job was to hold the Germans, at the same time acting as a pivot for the British and Canadian troops in the centre of the beach-head, and for the American troops on the extreme right. We did not know it then, but our flank—pooh-poohed by war correspondents as the ' phoney front '—was to become the hinge of the Allied force which finally swept on to Paris and Brussels.

6

On August 1 we took over our new sector from a battalion of the 3rd Parachute Brigade, about a mile and a quarter due south of our previous positions at Amfreville, in the area of the cross-roads at Le Mesnil, and on the extreme left of First S.S. Brigade's front.

The left flank re-shuffle had now resolved itself as follows. From Salanelles to Le Mesnil was held by units of Sixth Airborne Division, and the sector Le Mesnil-Troarn was held by the First and Fourth S.S. Brigades.

Our immediate neighbours were a battalion of the Oxfordshire and Buckinghamshire Light Infantry on our left, and 3 Commando on our right.

We were nearer to the enemy now in a static position than we had ever been before. Our forward posts were held by two fighting Troops only, who were changed over every seventy-two hours. Their positions were well dug in behind a high hedgerow overlooking a field, on the far side of which lay the enemy. In some parts of the area the distance between both sides was as little as fifty yards, whilst in others it varied from one hundred to a hundred and fifty yards. Commando headquarters was meanwhile set up in a large tile factory a little to the east of the cross-roads, together with the three-inch mortars and Vickers machine-guns.

Digging-in in the tile factory was not so easy, owing to the extremely hard nature of the ground. However, most of the men in headquarters managed to construct some sort of ' funk hole ' in the factory itself, under brick kilns, or with heavy, solid material they could find.

With our positions so close to the enemy, we naturally had to move about with extreme caution: in any case, before we had been at Le Mesnil any length of time we found ourselves being mortared and shelled by the enemy with extreme intensity and accuracy.

Commando headquarters caught the worst ' packet ' from this shelling and mortaring. All day long, at studied intervals—the enemy seemed to have a habit of bombarding us with especial ferocity at lunch and tea-time—we could hear the sharp popping sound of their mortars in the distance. When we heard it we knew that we had about half a minute to get under cover. At first, however, we suffered a number of casualties, mainly people who didn't seem to hear the warning sound that the bombs were coming. We therefore arranged with the Ox. and Bucks battalion on our left for a special ' mortar sentry ' whose job it was to blow a whistle at short intervals as hard as he could whenever he heard the mortars open fire.

Even after this precaution casualties persisted in slowly mounting up. They were chiefly sustained by the ration parties who went forward three times daily to the fighting Troops.

It was the same on the whole of the Brigade front, although our Commando seemed to be receiving the bulk of the mortar bombs, due no doubt to the fact that we were astride the all-important Le Mesnil cross-roads. These cross-roads also came under extremely demoralising shell-fire from heavy enemy guns believed to be situated on the high ground beyond the River Dives, well to the east. We took frequent sound bearings by compass when the shelling started, and although our information was passed back to the Gunners —who vainly tried to retaliate by putting down heavy concentrations on the Dives area—the shelling continued.

Meanwhile our own activities were confined entirely to sniping, patrolling, and counter-mortaring. Sniping was easy for us. We were close to the enemy, we had several expert shots in the unit, and the Germans seemed, for the most part, extremely careless in their movement. The result was that our snipers met with considerable success.

There was a somewhat quaint ritual observed by both sides regarding sniping. During the mornings the enemy only would snipe, having the sun behind them; in the afternoons the position was reversed, for the sun would be blinding the enemy. This procedure suited us down to the ground, for it gave us the whole morning to watch the Germans, noting those parts of the hedge where they showed themselves most. Thus, by the time afternoon came, we had placed our snipers accordingly, and were ready for the kill.

7

Nevertheless, it was a nerve-racking sort of war at Le Mesnil. Every day somebody or other was either killed or wounded by the enemy's incessant mortar fire, which we just couldn't seem to silence. The Germans became more active with their patrolling at night, too.

Towards the end of the first week in August a listening post fifty yards in front of Able Troop's area (they were doing their turn in the forward posts at the time) was attacked at one o'clock in the morning. The post, which was manned day and night by a standing patrol of a corporal and two men, was completely surprised. A party of Germans succeeded in crawling to within ten yards of the position, throwing grenades which killed one of the men and wounded the other. The corporal managed to escape, and made his way back to Commando headquarters with the news.

We were all furious when he had told us his story. Colonel Gray despatched a patrol immediately, with orders to try and intercept the enemy before they withdrew to the safety of their own lines. The patrol was not successful, for the enemy were nowhere to be found: but we were to have our revenge within a matter of days. . . .

For some time we had heard, regularly at eight o'clock on alternate evenings, the sound of a German vehicle drawing up to a farm a little way behind the enemy lines. As we were so close to each other at this period it was possible to hear, within a few minutes of the German vehicle's arrival, faint cries of feminine laughter floating on the evening breeze.

At first we did not know quite what to make of this. Many of us suspected the worst. The Germans were known to be in the habit of organising mobile brothels which toured their front-line areas for the delectation of their war-weary infantry. Whatever the purpose of these truckloads of ladies, however, it was quite obvious that the troops of 744 Infantry Regiment went in for gay front-line parties in a big way.

Colonel Gray decided, after the annoying attack on our listening post, that the time had come to put a stop to this sort of thing, German troops or no.

Accordingly, on the following evening, at a quarter to eight, he was to be found perched in the rafters of a large barn in the forward area, overlooking a considerable portion of the enemy's camp, including the farm in question. By his side sat a Gunner forward observation officer, who was in touch with a complete battery of 25-pounders. The Gunners, needless to say, had been informed of the nature of their target, and were rubbing their hands quite joyously at the prospect.

At eight o'clock, with its customary punctuality, the vehicle arrived, to be followed by the usual feminine giggles. A few minutes were allowed, in order that the enemy might 'get settled,' as Colonel Gray put it, then our work began.

For twenty minutes that farm received one of the heaviest shellings a single building could possibly have been subjected to. Afterwards the Colonel and the Gunner officer returned to Commando headquarters, satisfied men.

The German vehicle, needless to say, was never heard to call again. Our first attempt at moral uplift had been highly successful.

8

By the second week in August enemy mortaring had reached an almost unbearable pitch. They were firing bombs on an average of 400 a day along the whole of the Brigade front. Patrolling from our lines had to be drastically restricted, too, as the Germans had strengthened their positions by extensive wiring, mining and booby-trapping.

It was about this time that we heard of Peter Winston, for the first time since D Day. An Airborne corporal came crawling through one of our positions one night, and told us that he had succeeded in making his way through the

German lines from the outskirts of Troarn. According to him there were some forty Allied troops, including Peter Winston, several men of Sixth Airborne Division, and some British and American fliers, who had grouped themselves into an escape party, having made their way from a point near Trouville, on the French coast, many miles to the east. At the present moment they were hiding in some marshes near Troarn before splitting up into small parties, some of whom proposed to head for Spain, whilst others were wait- ing for the Allied advance to pass through them, so that they would automatically be freed.

This was great news. It meant, at least, that Peter Winston was alive, although there was nothing we could do to help him. We could only hope that, whatever course of action he decided upon, he would be successful and rejoin us unscathed.

By now British Second Army had launched a break-out from the hell that was Caen. A fierce battle was being fought at Falaise, where Allied tank formations had en- circled the bulk of the German Seventh Army. Conse- quently the enemy forces opposite Sixth Airborne Division and ourselves were now in serious danger of being outflanked from the south.

Nevertheless, these German troops that opposed us on the left flank showed no immediate signs of pulling out: but it was obvious that they would have to do so, sooner or later. Accordingly, a plan was drawn up by Sixth Airborne Division, with the two S.S. Brigades under command, to give chase to the enemy when they finally withdrew. It meant chasing them on foot, for neither the Airborne troops nor ourselves had very much in the way of transport. What little we had would be needed to carry heavy weapons, stores and ammunition.

However, we made ready for the chase. Orders were drawn up and explained to everyone. The code name given to the operation was ' Paddle.'

CHAPTER 6

PERIOD AUGUST 17—SEPTEMBER 2, 1944

On August 17, in the early hours of the morning, 'Operation Paddle' was launched. The enemy had withdrawn, very quietly and cleverly, during the night.

Whilst Numbers 3, 4 and 6 Commandos set off as rapidly as possible to follow up the Germans, we took over the whole of what had previously been the Brigade front, acting as 'firm base' should anything go wrong.

At eight o'clock, messages were received from 4 and 6 Commandos to the effect that the wooded areas to the east, together with the villages of Bavent and Robehomme, had been reached and cleared. No Germans had been found.

Meanwhile, in the heavily wooded Bois de Bavent, which ran many hundreds of yards south of Le Mesnil, the Brigade engineers were trying to blast their way through the one and only road which ran through the Bois, and which the enemy had successfully blocked with felled trees before making his retreat.

By two o'clock in the afternoon the information we had to hand showed that the enemy had withdrawn—more or less intact—to a fresh defensive line on the River Dives. Brigadier Mills-Roberts therefore ordered us to advance to Bavent, joining the remainder of the Brigade.

We reached Bavent late that evening, taking up a position to the north of the village. The night passed uneventfully, and when dawn broke on the following morning there was still no sign of the enemy, even on the far side of the Dives. The Brigadier commenced planning for an immediate crossing, ordering our Commando to carry out battle reconnaissance of a section of high ground beyond the river known as the Brucourt feature. This feature, incidentally, dominated all approaches to the river from our side.

With the unit's second-in-command, Major Ian De'Ath, in charge—he had joined us from England after the first few days of fighting at Amfreville—a patrol, consisting of the whole of Baker Troop, set out on this all-important reconnaissance. They crossed the Dives east of Robehomme by a partially demolished bridge, then proceeded northwards on a long and tedious march along the east bank of the river.

By clever exposure the patrol managed to draw sufficient fire from the enemy to be able to determine accurately the outline of the enemy's defences. This done, they withdrew back across the river, under painfully close shell-fire all the way.

The results of this reconnaissance proved of invaluable assistance to Brigadier Mills-Roberts in his plan for the crossing in strength. He now ordered Major De'Ath to carry out a second patrol, of a more supplementary nature, on the following morning, August 19, to examine possible crossing-places for the Brigade over the subsidiary streams, rivers and marshes beyond the Dives itself.

This second patrol never came off, however, for that same evening we crossed the river, proceeding to an assembly area previously determined near the village of Plain Gouchet.

F

Here the Brigadier issued his final orders. First S.S.
Brigade were to advance by night and outflank the enemy
now known to be holding the Brucourt feature. This was
to be done by a night infiltration through the German lines,
with the high ground in the area of the village of Angoville
as the Brigade's ultimate objective.

2

At one o'clock in the morning of the 20th the operation
commenced. The entire Brigade set forth from Plain
Gouchet in single file, Number 3 Commando leading. This
method of moving by night, following a white tape laid by
the leading element, was destined to become extremely well-
known to us in later battles—particularly in Germany. The
original idea of Brigadier Mills-Roberts for moving his men
at high speed by night, it rejoiced amongst the men in the
name of ' snake.'

The approach march was long, dismal, and more than
monotonous. It lasted for over four hours, during which
time we saw no enemy whatsoever. By five o'clock in the
morning we had passed through the German forward positions unobserved, and as dawn broke coldly and greyly
over the Brucourt-Angoville feature we had already started
to dig in.

Our objective had thus been reached without a fight.
Many people thought in consequence that the enemy had
withdrawn even further to the east than had first been
supposed. Others said that the Germans were there all
right, but we had surprised them. There would be a battle
later on.

The latter proved to be only too correct.

Before we had been digging an hour we heard the crackle of rifle and machine-gun fire to our immediate front. The Germans, undoubtedly still surprised, were beginning to rally themselves. Colonel Gray immediately took a party off with him on reconnaissance, to make ready for the inevitable attack. The rest of us dug harder and faster in the meantime. It wouldn't be long before the shelling started now, and we should all need good, deep slit trenches.

All of us were well dug in by half-past seven that morning, with 3 Commando on our left and 6 Commando on our right. 4 Commando had meanwhile arrived on their objective, a section of rising ground beyond 6 Commando. Brigadier Mills-Roberts ordered Colonel Gray to send out a patrol to make contact with 4.

Although the whole of Able Troop were despatched on this patrol it proved quite impossible to make any sort of contact. To reach them the Troop had to cross a shallow valley which they had originally covered during the night march. On their way over they suddenly found themselves 'pinned down' by the heavy fire of several intervening German strong-points, whose presence had hitherto been unknown. The patrol was only extricated from its unhappy plight by covering fire and smoke concentrations laid on by the Gunners ; and even then they lost their newly appointed Troop Commander, Bryan White, who was killed during the withdrawal.

As a result the Brigade now found itself with three Commando units securely entrenched in a tight defensive ring, whilst Number 4 was completely isolated.

Throughout the morning the Germans mortared and shelled us with great accuracy : and they did not end their activities here, for they often followed up their concentrations of fire with a series of counter-attacks. The first two came in against the Brigade right flank, directed in the main at the extreme left of 6 Commando and the right tip of our own, where Ian Beadle was entrenched with Easy Troop. Both these attacks were fortunately beaten off, with little loss to our men, the Germans sustaining the bulk of the casualties.

The third counter-attack was aimed at Able Troop, now commanded by Tommy Thomas, which had assumed the task of protecting Commando headquarters and generally covering the rear of the unit area on return from their abortive patrol earlier on. This attack was also beaten off, but not without heavy fighting, Tommy Thomas having picked off a number of the enemy with his rifle.

By midday the situation had quietened down a little, remaining so until the early afternoon, when Charlie Troop, under Captain Peter Barnard, were sent out to patrol the area forward of the Brigade positions. No Germans were encountered, and the Troop finally returned with a few badly wounded Germans who had been left by their comrades after the various counter-attacks.

Apart from intermittent shelling by the enemy's heavy guns the rest of the day was spent in comparative peace. Just before midnight a column of jeeps arrived at the Brigade positions, bringing much-needed food and ammunition from the other side of the Dives.

That night we should have slept, for there was no interference of any kind—as far as the Germans were concerned, anyway. But it seemed as if the heavens had conspired against us. We spent a fruitless, fretting night in the darkness, trying to sleep in the bottom of slit trenches which steadily filled with mud and water as the rain poured down relentlessly. Far away in the distance, too, we could hear the sounds of enemy transport, somewhere to the north, withdrawing east along the coastal roads leading to the Seine.

3

It was a cheerless dawn that broke the darkness in the early hours of the following morning: and in the still, cold half-light there were still no signs of an enemy who had become so curiously inactive since noon the previous day.

At ten o'clock a force under the command of Major De'Ath, consisting of Able and Baker Troops complete, together with a Gunner observation officer and a mortar mobile fire control party, set off to investigate the Brucourt feature which now lay behind us and which might, for all we knew, still be occupied by stragglers from the retreating German armies. A signal received from Ian De'Ath at mid-day told us, however, that the feature had been reached and occupied without opposition. A few odd Germans (who did not appear to know quite what was going on) had been made prisoner.

The rest of the day passed without further incident. By dusk we were concentrated in an area south of the main Varaville-Branville road, where Colonel Gray set up his headquarters in a former German supply dump, which was crammed to the roofs with discarded Wermacht equipment of every description.

Of course it wasn't very long before all the men had acquired some sort of souvenir for either Dad, Mum, or the 'pusher' (girl friend). All in all, we had quite a pleasant time.

On the following morning, August 22, we embussed in lorries which had been allotted to us by Sixth Airborne Division so that we could advance more speedily, and eventually arrived at a small village by the name of St. Vaast En Auge, some ten miles further east. Here we debussed, and no sooner had we done so than Colonel Gray received information from the Brigadier to the effect that a suspected German V2 dump lay in some woods to the east of the village, which we were to investigate. The dump was not officially described as ' V2 ' but as ' torpedo,' which was rather vague. However, as the former term had not yet come into use, such a description could readily be understood. In any case, whatever sort of a dump it was, the Germans were still believed to be occupying it, probably trying to evacuate their precious cargo.

Taking Baker, Charlie and Easy Troops with him, Colonel Gray set off for the dump. He hadn't got a very good idea as to its exact location, as he had no maps of the area in question, so he set off in what he hoped was the right direction.

Fortunately, the dump was successfully located, in a wood named the Bois de Villiers, not far from St. Vaast En Auge. It had long been evacuated, however, together with the torpedoes, V2s, or whatever they were, and it was a very disgruntled force, headed by an even more disgruntled Colonel, which finally rejoined the rest of us in the village late that night.

4

By now the battered remnants of the German Army were in full retreat from all sectors of the Allied beach-head. Great columns of transport, artillery and bewildered infantry were heading in a frantic stream towards the Seine.

Complete and utter victory for the Allies in Normandy was in sight. The sole resistance offered by the enemy now was coming from bands of isolated, desperate German troops, who were fighting for the most part purely in the hope of survival, having been told by their superiors of the awful fate which awaited them if they fell into Allied hands.

The next day, August 23, our advance continued. Once again we were ferried forward in the comparative comfort of lorries, reaching the town of Drubec by mid-afternoon. On arrival Colonel Gray was called to Brigade headquarters for further orders, whilst the rest of the unit made themselves as comfortable as possible in the bivouac areas allotted them.

It was significant that we now began to employ the term 'bivouac,' as opposed to 'digging in.' The Germans were in full flight. No longer was it necessary to prepare deep defensive positions every time we arrived at a place, then expect to have to hold it in the face of heavy shell-fire and repeated counter-attacks.

Colonel Gray did not return until eight o'clock that night. He came back, tired and dishevelled, with detailed plans for a night crossing of the nearby River Touques. The Commando was to cross at a point south of Pont L'Eveque and seize the high ground beyond.

The orders were passed on to the Troop Commanders, and from the Troop Commanders to the men. Once again weapons were hastily cleaned, ammunition checked, and stores issued. Just before midnight, however, the operation was cancelled. It would not be necessary to fight our way across the river. The Germans were not there, and consequently it would be far better to move in comfort and speed —by transport—the next morning, when the entire unit had been fully rested.

And so by noon the following day we had passed through Pont L'Eveque unopposed, and were again billeting ourselves in a fresh area—this time around a large chateau to the east of the town, formerly a German administrative headquarters.

No further orders were received until six o'clock that evening, when the advance continued. Our job this time was to infiltrate—in company with 6 Commando—through a series of enemy rearguard positions, and occupy the high ground to the west of the small town of Beuzeville, some twelve miles further east.

Within an hour the advance was under way, 6 Commando leading. As darkness drew on later in the evening the two units adopted ' snake ' formation—the usual long, stumbling, cursing column of men.

The march was uneventful until half-past ten that night. Then the leading Troop of 6 Commando walked smack into an enemy position. Both sides were disagreeably surprised, and a lot of confused firing followed ; but eventually the unexpected German opposition was overcome. Nevertheless, this small operation had held us up for over an hour, for the advance could not be continued until half-past eleven. At this stage a young Frenchman (member of the local Maquis) appeared from nowhere and offered to guide us through the German posiitons, which he claimed to know.

He led us for miles across country, over numerous obstacles, making a considerable detour to completely out-flank the enemy. The march was now complicated by the fact that it was extremely dark, and that we had already come a considerable distance before encountering the first enemy position. Everyone's reaction to this situation can easily be imagined. Tempers were running high, to say the least.

We did not rest until half-past four in the morning, when we halted for a short while to take over the lead from

6 Commando. It was always necessary to change over the lead during a long infiltration operation such as this, owing to the great strain placed on the nerves of those in front.

We wanted to reach our objective before first light, if possible, and as time was running short we increased pace and kept to the roads. The Frenchman's detour may have kept us out of trouble, but it had certainly wasted a lot of valuable time.

Signs of hastily evacuated German positions were passed on several occasions during the next half-hour, and two bedraggled-looking prisoners whom we pulled in *en route* told us that they belonged to a unit which had withdrawn only an hour or so before. These two Wermacht men, apparently, had had enough of war. They looked cold, tired, and hungry, and were only too pleased to give themselves up.

By great good luck we gained our objective on time. As we panted up the rising ground the first welcome gleams of dawn appeared in the dismal morning sky, whilst below us, just over the brow of the hill, lay the town of Beuze-ville.

5

Throughout the early part of the morning our new positions received most unwelcome attention from the enemy's mortars, which appeared to be firing from somewhere on our right flank. It was annoying to have to dig in again, after the comparatively comfortable bivouacs of the past few days, but it was just as well we did so, for the Germans around Beuzeville looked like making a stand.

Apart from the mortaring, the woods to our front began

suddenly to seethe with snipers who, with their customary lack of feeling, began to make all movement on our part distinctly unhealthy.

Just before midday Colonel Gray sent Tommy Thomas and Able Troop to reconnoitre the railway bridges which lay to the front of Beuzeville. The patrol returned in the afternoon, to report that these had been blown by the enemy. On their way back Able Troop had had the misfortune to encounter several German snipers and parties of somewhat determined stragglers, all of whom had put up a fight. The snipers, however, had been disposed in no uncertain manner, after which the Troop had proceeded to pass—in the words of Ian De'Ath, who interviewed Tommy Thomas upon his return—'with great aplomb, through that portion of the wood where enemy opposition was thickest.'

The rest of the day was spent in perfecting our positions, and awaiting any possible counter-attack. In the evening we contacted the local Maquis, whose enthusiasm for the offensive proved to be unbounded. Owing to the paucity of their equipment, however, they had to be restricted to matters of commissariat—as far as we were concerned, anyway.

Later on that evening it was decided to infiltrate one complete fighting Troop from both 6 Commando and ourselves through the German positions in the area of Beuzeville proper, and thus cut off any possible withdrawal on the part of the enemy to the east of the town.

The two Troops accordingly set out at one o'clock on the morning of the 26th. After the usual long and tedious march—due this time to the extensive detour that had to be made round Beuzeville—they finally arrived, some seven hours later, on their objective, establishing themselves astride the main German line of escape from the town.

But the enemy had beaten them to it. They had actually withdrawn about an hour beforehand. . . .

6

It was now obviously impracticable to chase the Germans any further. The Brigade was in a very depleted condition, with far less men and equipment than they had originally landed with on June 6.

Orders were received from Brigade headquarters that we were to have forty-eight hours' rest. We all positively whooped for joy. For the first time in eighty-two days we were going to be out of contact with the enemy, well beyond the range of their artillery, mortars, and Spandaus.

Our good fortune did not end here, either, for the ' forty-eight hour ' developed into a week, during which time the delights of nearby Beuzeville, Trouville and Honfleur were investigated, and—if the men's nightly condition was any judge—thoroughly appreciated.

Meanwhile the Wermacht were withdrawing as fast as they could across the Seine. British Second Army were following them up, but for us it was time to go home. We were no longer in any condition to fight.

On September 2 news was received from Brigade headquarters that the First S.S. Brigade, together with the Sixth Airborne Division, would be returning to England for a ' re-fit,' pending further operations.

Preparations for the move back commenced immediately, and four days later we were back at the original beach-head port of Arromanches. We sailed for England that night in tank landing craft, and the Channel crossing, to use the term employed by most people at the time, was perfectly bloody ; but the great thing was that we were going home.

So, in three short months, our first campaign had ended. We had learned many lessons, fought many bitter battles, lost many good men. There were the missing, too, Peter Winston, and the rest. What had become of them we did not know. We could only hope.

And then there was our future. This we did not know, either. Was it to be Italy, Burma, or North-West Europe again? One thing was certain. Our fighting days had not ended.

We had left behind us in France our comrades-in-arms, the men of the Fourth Special Service Brigade. This was but another mystery to us then, for no one knew why we had been pulled out and the Fourth Brigade left behind. However, within two months we were to know the reason why, for that Brigade had been earmarked for the bloodiest of all operations, the assault on Walcheren.

CHAPTER 7

PERIOD SEPTEMBER 8, 1944—JANUARY 13, 1945

BY September 7 we had reached our original marshalling area at Petworth, in Sussex. Twenty-four hours after we had been issued with fresh kit and bundled off on disembarkation leave.

Within a few days of our return later in the month to Petworth the entire Brigade was moved into civilian billets on the south coast. 3 and 6 Commandos found themselves in their old pre-D Day haunts in Brighton and Hove, but we were not quite so fortunate. Sufficient accommodation could not be found for us in Eastbourne, our original billeting area, so we went to Bexhill instead, which turned out to be just as good in the end. Brigade headquarters meanwhile established themselves at Lewes.

Number 4 Commando were not billeted anywhere. Within a few weeks of returning from disembarkation leave they found themselves on their way back to the Continent, to join 4 SS Brigade for the Walcheren operation. To compensate for the loss of 4, the Brigade was given Number 46 Royal Marine Commando in exchange.

Life in civilian billets was the best part of a Commando soldier's life. It was originally granted to Commando troops in the very early days of their formation, for two reasons. The first was that it was considered by the authorities to

be some slight reward for the hazardous work they were
doing ; and the second, to make them entirely self-reliant—
i.e., not living in a barrack-room, where the appropriate
N.C.O. would ensure they would arrive on parade in time,
etc. The importance of self-reliance in the Commando
soldier could never be over-emphasised, whilst the men, for
their part, appreciated billets far more than spending life in
barracks.

Commandos also received a special allowance, known as
Special Service Allowance (S.S.A.), to pay for their civilian
accommodation. The daily rate for officers—over and above
pay—was thirteen shillings, and for the men, six shillings.

2

We had not been in Bexhill very long before Peter
Winston rejoined us. Naturally, we were all extremely
pleased to see him, and to hear of his adventures since
D Day. For a long time, however, the fair-haired, tall,
broad-shouldered young subaltern refused to talk. In the
end, sitting in the Mess one evening, he eventually gave in
after persistent questioning, and told us the following story :

' Three weeks before D Day I was told that I would
accompany the Sixth Airborne Division as liaison officer for
the Brigade in the assault on Normandy. My fears of
possible failure—it would be my first operational jump—
were quietened a little when I learned that I would be travelling in the distinguished company of war reporters and
B.B.C. commentators. I felt that they were just as much
amateurs at the art of leaping out of aeroplanes as I was
myself !

' The weeks went quickly enough, with their incessant
briefings and rehearsals, and before we knew where we were

Brigadier the Lord Lovat, D.S.O., M.C.

Prelude to Invasion: Major-General R. E. ("Lucky") Laycock, the then Chief of Combined Operations, inspects the men of 45 Commando a few days before D Day. Standing immediately behind him are Lieutenant-Colonel N. C. Ries, Commanding Officer, 45 Commando, Major Nicol Gray, second-in-command, and Brigadier J. Durnsford-Slater, Deputy Commander, Special Service Group.

D Day: Men of First S.S. Brigade get ashore

D Day: Men of First Commando Brigade getting ashore

D Day: Men of First Commando Brigade moving inland from the beaches

The Left Flank: Lieutenant-Colonel Peter Young, C.O., of 3 Commando (right) gives final instructions to two of his snipers before they set out

Operation "Paddle" : 45 Commando enter Pont L'Eveque

The Rhine Crossing: 45 Commando enter the ruins of Wesel

Men of First Commando Brigade street fighting in Osnabruck

Osnabruck: Men of Baker Troop hoist their Troop flag in the city
It bears the Troop motto, "Bash On Regardless"

A Royal Marine Commando, a member of First Commando Brigade, looks back across the Elbe after the Brigade's successful (and final) river crossing in Northern Germany. April 1945

Victory in Germany, May 1945: Royal Marines Commando troops rest at the end of a campaign which has brought them from Normandy across NW Europe to the Baltic

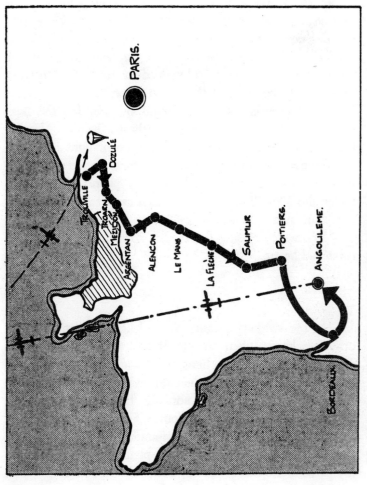

Map showing Lt. Peter Winston's Journey across France. The shaded area indicates the original Allied bridgehead

the time had come. We were waiting on the airfield, loaded with sixty pounds of equipment, tense and expectant.

'We took off from the airfield at dusk, some ten hours before the seaborne assault. As we glided low over the English Channel we could see the landing-craft, silhouetted in the moonlight as they put out to sea, thousands of tiny specks in the water, each speck representing a vessel crammed with men who had trained for four years to make the greatest operation of the war a success.

'England was soon left behind us, and for the next three hours there was nothing but the sea below. Nearing the French coast we ran into a tornado of light flak from the German beach defences. At the time we were only five hundred feet up, and could see very plainly the curving tracer and 20-millimetre shell-fire as it came towards, missing our plane by a miracle.

'We were crossing the French coast now. My adventures had begun.

3

'In the swaying Dakota the red light suddenly flashed on. We knew when we saw it that we had exactly ten seconds to go before we jumped. As we all stood up to get ready the green light flashed on, with equal suddenness. From then on it was pandemonium. Every man was trying to beat his comrades to the door. The next thing I knew was that I was in space . . . jumping . . . just a madly swirling body at the mercy of the plane's slipstream. Then my parachute opened: down, down, down. . . .

'I landed in a clump of large trees, and within five minutes or so succeeded in disentangling myself from the 'chute. Then I had a look round. Everything seemed peaceful after the turmoil of the jump—just trees and fields on all sides.

'I looked around for the men who had jumped with me, but could not see anyone. There was not, in fact, a single living thing to be seen. Nothing but trees and fields. Where was everyone else?

'The horrible truth gradually dawned upon me. I was alone.

'Ten minutes later a solitary glider passed overhead, about two hundred feet up. Its sides were ripped apart with flak, but it went on, and everything became deathly quiet again.

'To the east the sudden sound of firing broke the silence. It seemed very near—possibly only three or four hundred yards away. I learned later that in actual fact it was nearer a mile. I hurried towards the sound, hoping to find some of our own troops. As I walked along the path running along the edge of a field a figure suddenly loomed out of a nearby hedgerow. My fingers stiffened on the trigger of my Sten, but instead of firing I gave the password. A voice replied with the countersign in low, relieved tones. It was the voice of a parachutist corporal, lost like myself.

'We exchanged handshakes, held a rapid consultation, and decided to head north for the coast. We started to move rapidly across country which was completely unrecognisable from the air photographs we carried, our aim being to make contact with the seaborne troops, as we had obviously lost touch with our own comrades who had jumped with us.

'For the next hour or so we trudged across the countryside, and nothing happened. As we neared a main road running across our line of march we suddenly heard the sound of movement. Feverishly we threw ourselves into a ditch, and from our hiding-place saw a party of German cyclist troops, about 100 strong, go by. As soon as they had disappeared from view we moved on.

'Daylight came, and we had picked up three other para-chutists in the meantime, all of them victims of circum-stances similar to our own. The five of us—as we now were—hid for a short time in a thick copse, until we saw an old Frenchwoman walking across the fields. She didn't seem the least bit interested in us. Then I asked her, in halting French, where we were. I gathered from her reply that we were somewhere near Trouville, fifty miles east of our original objective!

'This was not the most depressing news the old French-woman gave us, either. Apparently we were surrounded by considerable numbers of Germans, all of whom were fully alive to the fact that the invasion of the Continent had begun.

'For the next five days we moved only in the hours of darkness, hiding the remainder of the time. The 24-hour rations we had jumped with were eked out with supplies of milk bought from the old Frenchwoman. During this period of hiding four more parachutists and a glider pilot joined our ranks. Our total number was now ten, including myself.

'On the afternoon of the sixth day, just as we were preparing to move off once more, we heard someone whist-ling "Tipperary," in unmistakable tones nearby. Looking out, I saw a Frenchman walking towards us. When he came up to our hiding-place he very politely introduced himself as Paul. As he spoke good English we found him easy to talk to, and after he had heard our story he implored us to let him take us to his house, where he could feed and hide us. We were only too glad to take advantage of his offer, and that night he guided us there.

4

'We stayed at Paul's for the next few days, and later that week he brought in five Canadian parachutists and a wounded glider pilot. Despite his entreaties to the contrary, I decided to try and slip through the German lines and reach our own troops.

'Paul could see that my mind was made up, so he did nothing more but try and help me. First of all a route was planned involving a lengthy tour to the south. This was highly necessary, as I wanted to avoid Dozule, a small French town, packed with German reserve troops at the time.

'I moved off with all the others who could possibly undertake the journey accompanying me. We could only travel short distances by night, being obliged—as was invariably the case—to hide by day. Paul, who also accompanied us, proved invaluable, providing us with all the information we required concerning enemy movements and dispositions. In addition to this he was able, as a civilian to travel ahead of us unhindered, selecting hiding-places for us, and arranging for food from his own friends in the district.

'It was at this stage of the proceedings that we learned of the existence of another party of parachutists who had been dropped from aircraft all over the place, like ourselves, and were also trying to make contact with the Allied troops. We decided to try and find them; but when we did so, we found that they were no better than we were. Amongst their number, incidentally, was a French-Canadian rear-gunner from a crashed Lancaster, who had made his way from a point some miles to the west of Paris!

'The two parties, numbering forty, now joined forces, camping a mile or so apart for security reasons. We were approximately three miles from the battle area now, and although it had been unanimously decided to try and rejoin our own troops rather than wait for the advance to liberate us, the difficulties to be overcome were immense. In the first place, we did not definitely know where our own troops were. We could only guess. Secondly, if we moved off and failed to make contact within two days or so, we should be cut off without food. Careful reconnaissance of the proposed route was therefore highly necessary, and this was carried out by a local member of the Resistance move-ment, the French-Canadian, and myself. (I had by now succeeded in obtaining a suit of civilian clothes, together with the requisite identity papers. The latter had been carefully faked, my father's photograph passing as my own.)

'Our position was now one mile south-west of Troarn. Two days previously a R.A.F. squadron-leader, who had crashed near Falaise, and the American pilot of a Thunder-bolt which had crashed near Dozule, joined us. We still lay hidden, and after a further four days' reconnaissance—which revealed that it would be quite impossible to move a party of our size to the British lines—decided upon a change of plan. This seemed highly expedient, especially as a large number of German infantry had suddenly encamped themselves in the field adjoining ours.

'We held a council of war, at which everyone was given an opportunity to state their views, and decide what they wanted to do. About fifteen were prepared to make a dash for the British lines, working in pairs. Eight decided to head for Spain (including myself), whilst the remainder were now either for staying where they were until the Allied advance caught up with them, or working their way round to the American sector, which might provide an easier route of escape.

'All the available maps, compasses, money and food were accordingly pooled and divided. Civilian clothes were found for those heading for Spain, and such weapons as we had were given to those making a dash to the British and American lines in uniform.

'On the evening of July 4, having been together for almost one month, we split up into our various parties. In many ways it was a dramatic moment, for obviously none of us knew which party would be successful, or which would fail.

5

'Of the parties heading south for Spain, all had members who could speak French. My particular party was a small one—very small, for it consisted of the squadron-leader who had joined us at Troarn and myself only. The danger lay, as far as we were concerned, in the fact that the squadron-leader had no identity papers. Consequently both of us kept well clear of the roads for the first day, looking innocent enough in our guise as farmhands, or *cultivateurs*.

'At four o'clock on the afternoon of the 5th we reached the town of Mezidon, where we spent the night in a large double bed which we had found in a bombed-out house. How grateful we were for that bed. It was the first we had slept in since D Day.

'The next day we pushed on towards Argentan, twenty-five miles away, following the main-line railway. We had to make frequent detours to avoid the huge craters caused on the line by R.A.F. bombers, and a mile and a half outside the town we found a quiet hayloft in a deserted farmyard, where we spent the night. At ten o'clock the next morning we passed through Argentan itself, on our way to Alencon, the next place of any importance on our route.

'There was not a single living thing in Argentan when we got there. The railway sidings and marshalling-yards were completely wrecked, the station was almost unrecognisable, and the streets were filled with the shells of buildings, no longer habitable after the battering they had received. The R.A.F. had, in fact, reduced Argentan to dust and ashes.

'We continued to walk along the railway line towards Alencon. Near the small town of Sees we were stoppped by a German sentry, who sprang out upon us from a small house beside a level-crossing to demand, in perfect French, who we were and where we were going.

'I explained that we were refugees from Falaise, and that we were trying to reach relatives in Alencon. After examining our papers—the squadron-leader had been fitted out with these by the very co-operative Mayor of Mezidon—the German allowed us to proceed, warning us to keep off the railway line. This we weren't at all sorry to do, as we had covered about sixty miles in this manner, stumbling along the line of the track from sleeper to sleeper.

'That night, by great good fortune, we came across a member of the local Resistance who put us up for the night. The next morning he insisted upon taking us to a wood five miles away, where four Allied airmen were hidden. One of these turned out to belong to the same squadron as the squadron-leader. He had been shot down a week previously, and the squadron-leader had thought him killed in action.

'However, it was impossible for us to move with any degree of safety through enemy territory if we increased the party in numbers, so we rather reluctantly left the four airmen in the wood and continued the journey to Alencon alone.

'We finally arrived in this town without further mishap, meeting the leader of the local Resistance, who promised us transport to help us on our way. The transport turned out to be a fire-engine, which the Resistance leader explained was the only vehicle which could be run under the very noses of the Germans without arousing undue suspicion.

'Donning firemen's helmets we started the fire-engine up, travelling for some thirty miles aboard it along the main highway leading to Le Mans, and ringing the fire bell at regular intervals very loudly and quite unnecessarily into the bargain. For some extraordinary reason the German troops who saw us never bothered to check the purpose of our journey. In fact the only upsetting factor throughout the entire proceedings was the number of inquisitive R.A.F. fighters overhead!

'By prearranged plan the fire-engine dropped us at a house five miles outside Le Mans, whose occupants supplied us with two cycles to continue our journey. We passed through Le Mans that afternoon whilst an air raid was in progress, and pushed on towards La Fleche, which was reached just before nightfall, spending the night in a farmhouse on the outskirts of the town.

'The next two days were comparatively uneventful. Progress was slowed down considerably, owing to the excessive number of punctures which our cycles received. As we had no repair outfits with us it necessitated frequent hunts for *mechaniciens,* who more often than not were many miles off our route.

' In this way we moved through Saumur to Poitiers. It
was now July 15, and we had already covered nearly three
hundred miles of our journey to Spain.

6

' Once past Poitiers we began to enter the Maquis country. Here we were stopped at frequent intervals by German
patrols, who proved to be by far the most suspicious we had
yet encountered. That night, as was our custom, we
approached a house and asked for water—this was always
our preliminary question when seeking a bed for the night.

' As I stood on the doorstep and talked to the occupant
of the house, an old man, I could hear the B.B.C. news in
French coming through very faintly from London. I immediately disclosed the identity of both the squadron-leader
and myself. The old Frenchman, however, was extremely
suspicious, and we had to spend the rest of the evening
convincing him that we were British. Once satisfied, he put
us up for the night, directing us the next morning, through
devious channels, to the headquarters of the local Maquis.

' But our troubles were not yet over. Most of the local
inhabitants—themselves members of the Maquis—suspected
us of being Gestapo agents. After a lot of hard work we
eventually succeeded in convincing them also that we were
British, and so found ourselves in the local Maquis headquarters. Here we were obliged to stay for a whole week,
for the Maquis insisted on providing a guide—to be sum-
moned from Bordeaux—to conduct us on the remainder of
our journey.

' The guide duly arrived after a week, and we departed
by train, in brand-new suits of civilian clothes, to Bordeaux.
Our instructions were to feign sleep whilst in the train, and

do whatever our guide did. All went well until we were about thirty miles from Bordeaux, where everyone was ordered to change trains. To our dismay we found that the new train was nothing more than a German troop train, on which civilians had been permitted to travel! However, apart from at attempt by the Maquis to wreck the train *en route,* we arrived at Bordeaux quite safely and followed our guide on to a tram which took us into the suburbs of the city. Here we were to stay until we could catch another train running south to the Spanish border.

'We learned later, however, that this particular railway line running to Spain had been sabotaged—presumably by the Maquis—and so we had to prolong our stay in Bordeaux. The local Resistance eventually decided to move us by car to a point twenty miles south of the town, where we could pick up a train. Accordingly, on the morning of August 4 we met the car at a prearranged rendezvous, and started off on our journey. We reached the centre of the town, and were driving along one of the main streets when a cordon of Gestapo agents appeared from nowhere and threw themselves across the road, forming a solid line which blocked our path completely. Without further ado we found ourselves being unceremoniously bundled out of the car, then marched off to Gestapo headquarters with our hands above our heads.

'We had been trapped. Unfortunately for us, as we afterwards learned, the head of the local Resistance movement was also head of the Gestapo in Bordeaux.

7

'At Gestapo headquarters we were grilled with typical German thoroughness and ingenuity. The usual tricks were

employed—face-slapping, refusal to recognise us as prisoners
of war, threats of death if we didn't " talk," and statements
waved in our faces purporting to have been signed by our
accomplices which revealed our " true " identity.

' We revealed no information. The Gestapo accordingly placed us in solitary confinement, in small cells twenty
feet underground. Further interrogation followed, after
which we were transferred to Bordeaux gaol. Here we
were joined by six American fliers, tricked into capture by
exactly the same ruse as we had been.

' We spent nearly three weeks in the gaol, our food
during this period consisting mainly of bread and soup.
Every day Allied airmen who had been shot down in the
area were being brought in, and by August 12 Allied
prisoners totalled nineteen.

' Thanks to the American break-through at Nantes, and
the crossing of the River Loire, however, the Gestapo
evacuated the gaol, heading back to Germany at full speed :
but before they did so they handed us over to the Luftwaffe
at Bordeaux-Merignac aerodrome. We stayed another five
days here, but the treatment we received at the hands of
the Luftwaffe was infinitely better than that of the Gestapo.

' On the night of August 26, having completely wrecked
the aerodrome, the Luftwaffe also evacuated Bordeaux and
headed for Germany, taking us with them. For three days
and nights we travelled in lorries, covering a distance of
almost one hundred miles inland. During this period one
of our fellow prisoners fell sick, and was placed in the
civilian hospital at Angouleme. The next day we all feigned
sickness, claiming that we had contracted ptomaine poison-
ing. To our amazement the German doctor attached to the
Luftwaffe believed us, placing us all in the same hospital
as the fellow who had fallen sick the day before.

' That night the Luftwaffe's lorries moved out, and the next morning we made contact with the leader of the local Maquis. This proved easy enough, for by this time more than half the town had been liberated—the remaining Germans had not the slightest interest in fighting—and was under their control. We were still far from home, however, for a retreating German army lay between us and the Allied forces. On the night of September 2 help came at last from an unexpected quarter. Without any previous warning whatsoever the Maquis suddenly transported us to an unknown spot in the surrounding countryside, where two American supply planes, operating in conjunction with the French Resistance movement, were expected to land. At two o'clock in the morning they finally arrived.

' Four and a half hours later the squadron-leader and myself touched down on an airfield.

' England was beneath our feet.'

PART TWO

HOLLAND

CHAPTER 8

PERIOD JANUARY 15—JANUARY 22, 1945

THE months in England soon passed. Christmas came and went : but there was still no definite news of our future. We had heard, it was true, various tales as to where we *might* be sent—the most persistent being that we were due to embark for the Far East ' almost any day now.' To supplement this rumour a lot of the senior officers in the unit started to become very jungle-minded, and in consequence everyone received a positive spate of lectures on jungle warfare and conditions generally in Burma and the Pacific.

In addition to this we had already carried out a considerable amount of field training on the South Downs, for we had had to train as a unit once more, having received numbers of reinforcements during the past few months to bring us up to battle strength.

There had been several changes amongst the officers in the Brigade. As far as our Commando was concerned, Colonel Gray still remained as C.O., but we had lost our second-in-command, Major Ian De'Ath, D.S.O. He had been posted to Italy as Brigade Major of the Second Special Service Brigade, and in his place came Major ' Ben ' de Courcy-Ireland.

Bill Neaves still remained as Adjutant of the unit, but we had a new doctor sent to us. His name was John

Tulloch, and he was a young, quiet Scotsman who was later to prove one of the stalwarts of the Commando. Our former doctor, Hugh Smith, went to Number 10 (Inter-Allied) Commando.

As far as the fighting Troops were concerned, Able Troop was now commanded by Captain Dudley Coventry, a regular Army officer of immense physique, who had been connected with the Commando movement since the earliest days of its formation: Baker Troop was commanded by John Day, duly promoted from subaltern to Captain; Charlie Troop by Peter Barnard, who took over the Troop in Normandy; Dog Troop—almost completely re-formed—by Major ' Bunny ' Kirby; and last, but by no means least, Easy Troop—still commanded by the redoubtable Ian Beadle.

The Heavy Weapons Troop (mortars and machine-guns) continued under the able direction of Colin Fletcher, who had taken over command from Bill Neaves when the latter became Adjutant.

During our stay in England one or two additional decor-ations for the unit had also come through. Colonel Gray received a D.S.O., Ian Beadle and Tommy Thomas the M.C., whilst a few of the men were awarded the M.M.

It was about this time that we were told that the name of our formation was to be changed. No longer were we to be known as Special Service troops. Instead of calling our Brigade ' First Special Service Brigade,' we were now to be known as ' First Commando Brigade.'

There were two main reasons for this official change in designation, apparently. The first was that, for our Ameri-can allies, the term ' Special Service ' meant something that was their equivalent to E.N.S.A. The second—and this probably the more likely—was that British ' S.S.' troops on the Continent were likely to cause the wrong impression in newly liberated countries.

On the first Sunday after the New Year we carried out what was to be our final exercise in England before going forth to the wars again.

It was bitterly cold throughout the whole of that day, with snow lying thick on the Downs. Nevertheless, the entire unit practised battle procedure over and over again, until Colonel Gray was satisfied. At the end of it all he called us together, and told us that the Brigade had the highest priority for an operational move overseas, and that we could expect to be leaving the country in the near future.

A week later we were packing our bags and preparing to leave our comfortable billets in Bexhill. Our destination was Holland.

2

On January 15, we disembarked at Ostend, after a two-day crossing of the Channel from Tilbury. We stayed in a transit camp for a couple of days, then learned that the Brigade had been placed under command of 15 (Scottish) Division, with the task of holding conisderable stretches of the River Maas, across which it was hoped to patrol fairly extensively.

Our Brigade now consisted of Numbers 3, 6, 45 (Royal Marine) and 46 (Royal Marine) Commandos. Unfortu-nately, the Brigade was split on arrival at Ostend, 46 Com-mando being detached from the rest of us for special anti-parachutist duties at Antwerp, where it was thought the

Germans might attempt an airborne landing in their efforts
to recapture a port for themselves. Number 3 Commando
were detached, too, for they found themselves moved up to
the front within twenty-four hours of disembarking, to come
under command of the Eleventh Armoured Division on the
Maas, in the Stevensweerd area.

Meanwhile 6 Commando and ourselves moved up to
Baarloo, some miles north of Stevensweerd, where we came
directly under the command of 15 (Scottish) Division.
Although both Commando units totalled under 1,000 men,
we were nevertheless expected to relieve two complete
Scottish infantry battalions who had precisely double our
numbers.

Whilst this change-over was taking place we received no
interference from the enemy on the other side of the river.
It was just as well, for conditions were bitter, the snow being
very thick on the ground, whilst both sides were forced to
live out of slit trenches as much as possible, in such buildings
as were available.

We remained in Baarloo less than a week, then found
ourselves relieved by a battalion of our old friends the Sixth
Airborne Division, who had preceded our arrival in Holland
by a month or so, and had just concluded a particularly
bloody series of battles in the Ardennes.

We were not sorry to leave Baarloo, even though the
enemy had been reasonably quiet. It was too cold to patrol
the Maas by swimming across it, and boats for a similar
operation simply could not be obtained, so we had had to
just content ourselves with merely hanging about, manning
positions against an enemy whom we could not even see, and
keeping ourselves warm.

There had been but one brush with the Germans during

our stay at Baarloo. A small party of them had tried to cross the river one night in a rowing-boat. We, however, had seen them almost as soon as they pushed off from the bank, so that we waited until they were exactly half-way across, then opened up with a Bren gun. The boat was sunk, and its occupants believed drowned.

The Germans made no attempt to cross again.

3

On January 22 we moved south from Baarloo, to concentrate with 3 and 6 Commandos in the area of the town of Echt, where we found ourselves placed under a fresh divisional command—that of the Seventh Armoured Division 'Desert Rats.'

The tasks given us by the Divisional Commander were, firstly, to straighten out the 'bulge' on the divisional left flank—a large area of ground between the Roermond railway and the Maas ; and secondly, to capture the villages of Maasbracht and Brachterbeek, and the town of Linne. For these operations a squadron of tanks from the Royal Tank Regiment would be placed under our direct command, whilst fire support would be provided by a regiment of the Royal Horse Artillery. The Eleventh Hussars would also assist us on our right flank.

The operation commenced at eight o'clock on the morning of January 23. 6 Commando led the Brigade advance, followed by ourselves, with Brigade headquarters and 3 Commando in rear.

At first very little happened. We marched for over an hour and a half in the snow towards Maasbracht, meeting not the slightest opposition—not even shell-fire. Meanwhile, on our right we could hear the Hussars' tanks moving up— a most heartening sound.

By a quarter to ten 6 Commando had entered Maas-bracht. The place was completely deserted. The enemy had obviously withdrawn the night before, for they had been observed moving about in the village on the previous day.

A few minutes later we followed 6 Commando through the village, the usual long, single file of silent men, our steps making little noise in the crisp, flaky snow, which dazzled the eye wherever one looked. The air was fresh and clean, and it was difficult to believe that somewhere before us an alert, hard-fighting enemy lay in wait, determined to give battle.

We travelled on to Brachterbeek, which adjoined Maas-bracht. By this time 6 Commando had ' fallen out,' to occupy Maasbracht, and we were now heading the Brigade column.

Brachterbeek was also found to be deserted. There was not even a Dutch man, woman, or child around who might have given us any information. It all seemed horribly ominous, this quietness, with no one in sight for miles, and nothing but great flat sheets of snow carpeting the country-side.

Brigadier Mills-Roberts ordered us to push on to Linne, which lay some three thousand yards due east of Brachter-beek. Led by Dudley Coventry and Able Troop we in-creased pace, heading for the railway station, which lay just beyond the main road leading into the town.

On reaching a road junction some two hundred yards short of the station, however, Able Troop suddenly came under intense enemy mortar and machine-gun fire. They

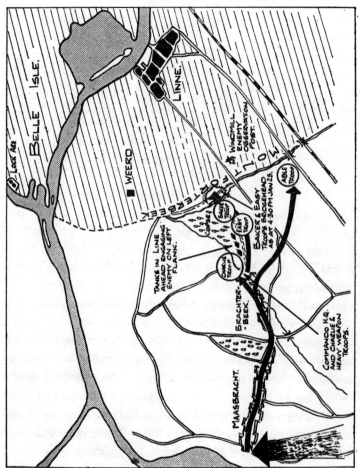

The Brachterbeek action. Shaded area indicates enemy territory

dashed for cover on either side of the road, only to be pinned down ' where they lay by devastating shell-fire.

The Germans had sprung a very clever trap.

4

Our advance towards Linne had been spotted by the enemy almost as soon as we had entered Brachterbeek, and they had waited for us accordingly. Their defences were particularly strong, for they were holding—as far as we could estimate—a line running roughly behind the Mort-forterbeek, a long dyke which extended from the railway station due north to De Villa.

Whilst Able Troop were having their work cut out to hold their own down at the station, the rest of us came under heavy shell-fire in the Brachterbeek area. By this time, however, we had already taken up rough defensive positions in the village, holding a line from the north-east of Brachterbeek—where we had been fortunate in discovering some very well-dug German trenches which had been abandoned —to the cross-roads at Chap.

Down at the station Able Troop were completely cut off by now. Colonel Gray had made several attempts to withdraw them back to the village under cover of smoke put down by the Artillery, but each one had proved abortive. Every time the smoke burst forth from expended shell-cases into a spiralling screen the enemy increased their mortar, machine-gun and shell-fire accordingly. They had also succeeded by now in bringing up several self-propelled guns, which were being used to great effect, both on Able Troop and upon Commando headquarters in Brachterbeek.

As it was literally impossible for Able Troop to carry out any sort of organised withdrawal, Colonel Gray sent a wireless message to Dudley Coventry, ordering him to hold his present position until nightfall, when his Troop was to withdraw to Brachterbeek. Colonel Gray also gave orders for the troop of tanks from the Royal Tank Regiment to move round on the left flank and engage enemy positions from De Villa to as far north as possible, thus covering the future deployment of any of our fighting Troops on that flank.

The tanks rumbled out of Brachterbeek to take up their positions. As soon as the Germans heard them they put down an immense concentration of fire on the village. Fortunately there were no casualties. The tanks steadily worked their way up in line ahead along a narrow gully running straight towards the Montforterbeek ; and once in position they commenced engaging suspected enemy build-ings with a vengeance, filling the air with the steady pumping sound of shells fired from the guns in their turrets, and the orange-coloured wisps of tracer machine-gun bullets.

Under cover of this fire Easy Troop also moved round on the left, working their way forward to a copse two hundred yards short of the Montforterbeek. Here they were joined within a matter of minutes by Baker Troop, under John Day.

Whilst Baker Troop had been moving up to join Easy Troop, Ian Beadle had crawled forward even further, on reconnaissance. He returned, unfortunately, with but little information. The enemy appeared to be in strength in a gully to the immediate front of the copse, just beyond the Montforterbeek, but that was as much as he had been able to ascertain.

As he was temporarily out of contact with Colonel Gray at Commando headquarters, Ian Beadle assumed command of the two Troops in the copse, and gave orders for the

* German sub-machine-gun.

attack on the Montfortenbeek, and the gully lying beyond it. Baker Troop were to carry out a flanking movement to the left, actually assaulting the gully, whilst Easy Troop supported them with fire, later following up the attack to form a second wave.

It was a bloody battle which followed, for the gully was only reached in the face of intense enemy fire, and through the bravery and leadership of Peter Riley, a young subaltern who hailed from Guernsey attached to Baker Troop, and Sergeant Noakes, of the same Troop.

Together with Sergeant Noakes, Peter Riley led the first wave of Baker Troop's assault upon the gully. They captured two machine-gun posts, killing all the Germans within range with grenades and tommy-gun fire.

The time was now half-past two in the afternoon. There had been no time for food, and all of us had been lying in the snow for hours, and were frozen with the cold. Meanwhile, back at Commando headquarters in Brachterbeek, heavy shelling of the area by the German self-propelled guns had been going on for some time, and causing not a little trouble. We had sustained many casualties here, including Peter Barnard, the commander of Charlie Troop, which had been acting as protection unit to Commando headquarters since their arrival in the village.

To reinforce his bridgehead over the Montforterbeek, Coloney Gray committed his last available Troop—Dog Troop, under Major Kirby, and with Peter Winston as one of its subalterns. This Troop moved up along on the left flank, past the tanks, and over the beek to join Baker Troop in the gully, where the latter were well dug in by now. Easy Troop had meanwhile taken up a position in the copse which lay between Commando headquarters and the gully.

Down at the station Able Troop's plight was still as bad as ever. The entire area was continually being raked with enemy machine-gun fire, and the slightest move spelled death in consequence. Casualties to the Troop had steadily mounted during the day, and unless something could be done for them it was feared that many would die.

It was here that John Tulloch, the doctor, came to Able Troop's aid. Collecting together every available jeep he could possibly lay his hands on, he led a convoy from Brachterbeek down to the station in broad daylight, under cover of the Red Cross, to evacuate the wounded.

Unlike a similar occasion in Normandy, the Red Cross was not respected by the Germans. The convoy was, in fact, subjected to the most intense fire imaginable, down the whole length of the road running from the cross-roads at Chap to the station. Despite this, Tulloch reached Dudley Coventry's headquarters with all his jeeps intact, and succeeded in getting the wounded back to Brachterbeek, where they were evacuated to base hospital through the usual medical channels.

For this gallant work he was later awarded the Military Cross.

5

The battle of the Montforterbeek had been one of the bloodiest we had ever struck, Normandy included. The worst part about it was the bitter weather, which gave several of the men severe frostbite. The Germans in front of us, too, were putting up a desperate fight against odds, although they had had the advantage in the first instance of well-prepared defensive positions which had surprised us earlier in the day.

Many received medals for the Montforterbeek action ; but none was more deserved than the Victoria Cross (posthumous) gained by Lance-Corporal Eric Harden, of the Royal Army Medical Corps, attached to 45 Commando.

Harden was Able Troop's medical orderly. During the morning's fighting at the station a section under command of one of the Troop subalterns—Lieutenant Robert Cory— was caught in the open country around the station by enemy Spandau fire. Although the section dashed for what little cover was available, as soon as the Germans had opened up Lieutenant Cory and two of his men had fallen where they stood, severely wounded.

Back at Able Troop headquarters Harden heard of these casualties. He immediately decided to go forward alone, crawling in the snow across the one hundred and twenty yards of flat, open ground which separated him from the three wounded men. For the whole of that distance he was continually fired on by the Germans with mortars and machine-guns.

Harden eventually reached the casualties, then calmly proceeded to dress their wounds. After that he lifted one of the Marines, and as he half carried him back to Com- mando headquarters bullets could be seen striking the snow all round him.

He reached the headquarters, taking the wounded Marine to a place of safety. Although already wounded in the side, he defied orders not to go out again, and organised a stretcher party, consisting of himself and two others, to bring in Lieutenant Cory and the remaining wounded man, thus making a further two trips across the fire-swept snow to bring them in. On the third trip, whilst returning with Lieutenant Cory, this fearless soldier was shot through the head.

Troop Sergeant-Major Bennet, of Able Troop, immediately dashed out from behind cover to assist, carrying both Cory and Harden back to Troop headquarters, where they were attended to by John Tulloch: but Harden was dead.

6

For the rest of that day we held grimly on, despite the unabating shell-fire and the bitter cold, and at a quarter-past seven in the evening the following message arrived from Brigadier Mills-Roberts:

Special Order of the Day. To all ranks, 45 Commando. The Divisional Commander congratulates 45 Royal Marine Commando on their valuable work to-day, which has been of great importance in driving back the enemy on the Divisional front. Well done, Royal Marines! You put up a fine show to-day, and I am very proud of you.

Three-quarters of an hour later, under cover of darkness, Able Troop finally managed to withdraw intact from the station. On reaching Commando headquarters in Brachterbeek Colonel Gray ordered them into immediate reserve, and to rest all night, after an extremely arduous day's fighting.

All was quiet until half-past nine that night, when Baker Troop, still manning the gully beyond the Montforterbeek, reported a determined counter-attack from the south. The Germans—who seemed to have rallied themselves and sallied forth from the Windmill—came in shouting and screaming for the blood of 'dirty British Commandos,' firing off all their weapons in a desperate attempt to demoralise our men.

Thanks mainly to Peter Riley, the attack was beaten off, with the inevitable heavy casualties to the enemy. Peter

Riley led his section of men out of their slit trenches in the
dark, to meet the S.S. troops hand to hand in the snow.
After the battle twelve bodies were counted, and it is known
that several more were wounded, the whole of the attacking
force being put to flight.

This short, bitter engagement proved to be the Germans'
last attempt to throw us out of the footing we had gained
over the Montforterbeek. Apart from occasional shelling
and mortaring the rest of the night passed without further
incident.

At six o'clock on the following morning, January 24,
we were relieved by Number 6 Commando, who came up
from Maasbracht. We accordingly marched out of the line
to the billets they had vacated for a twenty-four-hour rest.

7

So ended our first battle in Holland. Casualties had been
fair, considering the desperate nature of the fighting, and the
bitter weather conditions. The actual figures were twenty-
five killed and twenty-seven wounded.

The lowness of our casualties said much for the training
of the unit, for without a doubt, troops who had not been
trained to such a high standard as ourselves, meeting such
a determined enemy in such open country, would have
inevitably suffered a far worse fate.

CHAPTER 9

PERIOD JANUARY 23—JANUARY 29, 1945

THROUGHOUT January 24 we rested in billets in Maasbracht, where sleep soothed the mind and warmth the limbs
for the first time in over twenty-four hours.

The men, their faces blackened with mud and filth, and
frozen stubble on their chins, crawled wearily to rest anywhere in the buildings allotted them in the village—under
chairs and tables, on mattresses resurrected from the debris
of shell-torn houses, on benches, on piles of littered books in
school-rooms. Anywhere that would permit them to stretch
their legs and aching backs.

Brigadier Mills-Roberts had ordered that we were to
have complete rest, and so be fit for battle on the following
day. Whilst we slept peacefully in Maasbracht 6 Commando were busy consolidating our gains over the Montforterbeek, clearing the whole of the original German
defence line from De Villa to the railway station. By the
end of the day they were able to report that all enemy
resistance in the area of the beek had been overcome, and
that contact had been made south of the station with the
2nd battalion of the Devonshire Regiment.

2

At half-past seven on the morning of the 25th we were

preparing for battle again. The task given us this time was to support a combined tank and infantry attack on the Brigade's final objective—Linne. The tanks would be those of the Desert Rats, and the infantry, Numbers 3 and 6 Commandos.

It was a cold, grey morning, and as we marched through Brachterbeek we could see the town of Linne already burn-ing in the distance after heavy shelling by the Royal Artillery, with red flames licking billowing clouds of dirty, blackish smoke, contrasting sharply with the dazzling brightness of the soft white carpet of snow.

We passed the cross-roads at Chap, then turned left, to march due east along the road leading over the Mont-forterbeek, and eventually into Linne itself. Meanwhile Colonel Gray had moved on ahead of us, and was busy at that moment in conference with the Brigadier beside the Windmill, which commanded an excellent view of the town.

It was decided to send a force of two fighting Troops from 45 Commando to support the main attack by 3 Com-mando—which was about to begin—and that our second-in-command, Major de Courcy-Ireland, should be in charge.

The time was now twenty minutes past eight. Moving on the backs of tanks, 3 Commando penetrated the outskirts of Linne without encountering any opposition. A message received from them a little later stated that Dutch civilians in the town all reported that the Germans had withdrawn the night before.

If this was the case, it was obvious that the enemy had fallen back on their much-vaunted Siegfried Line, the outer defences of which lay only a mile or so beyond Linne. These defences, consisting of a maze of anti-tank ditches, communication trenches, barbed-wire obstacles and strong-points, were known as the ' Siegfried switchline,' or—to give the popular abbreviation—the ' Siegfried switch.'

The Brigadier now ordered Major de Courcy-Ireland to take his two-Troop force into the town to follow up 3 Commando's entry. Able and Charlie Troops accordingly went in under the Second-in-Command, and they also met with no opposition.

By ten o'clock that morning the whole of Linne had been cleared. 3 Commando remained in occupation of the town, except for the Church area in the north-east, which was taken over by Able and Charlie Troops. The remainder of our unit consolidated in the area as follows:

Baker and Easy Troops moved out north to the house known as De Weerd ; Dog Troop occupied a stretch of the De Villa-Linne road ; the Heavy Weapons' Troop took over the Windmill ; and Commando headquarters set themselves up in De Villa proper. Number 6 Commando meanwhile established themselves in the vicinity of the railway station.

The Brigade's victory was complete.

3

The rest of the day was spent digging in, and generally perfecting our new defensive positions. During the afternoon someone reported ' suspicious movement' along the banks of the Maas to our left, opposite Belle Isle. A patrol from Charlie Troop went out to investigate, but no signs of the enemy could be found.

It was now perfectly clear that the Germans, to our immediate front and right flank, anyway, had withdrawn to the fastnesses of the ' Siegfried switch.' Information regarding the left flank, however, was not quite so definite. We did not know for certain whether Belle Isle—so named by us, after the naval battle of 1761—was clear of the enemy or not. Accordingly, at three o'clock on the morning of January 26, a small reconnaissance patrol, consisting of three men under the command of Tommy Thomas, set out to cross the fast-flowing Maas in two two-men rubber dinghies. Half-way across the river they came under unpleasantly accurate rifle and machine-gun fire, and being too weak in numbers to make an opposed landing, withdrew as rapidly as possible.

Well, at least we knew that the Germans occupied the island. The next task was to find out how strong they were.

For the next forty-eight hours daylight standing patrols were sent out by Colonel Gray to man the river bank. All enemy movement was noted and carefully collated. The Germans appeared to have their forces in strength at the western end of the island, not facing us—we were on their southern flank—but rather facing Number 46 Commando, who had by now rejoined the Brigade from Antwerp.

Meanwhile, Colonel Gray had been told that information was required by the Commander of Seventh Armoured Division concerning enemy forces in Merum, a small town lying north of Belle Isle. To obtain such information it would mean crossing the Maas, marching across Belle Isle, and then re-crossing the river to the bulge of land south-west of Roermond. 45 Commando were given this task by the Brigadier, who placed a detachment from 10 (Inter-Allied) Commando under our direct command for the operation.

Very great care was taken by Colonel Gray over the planning of these two raids on Belle Isle and Merum, for they were both going to be tricky ones, to say the least. The operation was finally scheduled to take place on the night of January 27/28, and briefly the plan of attack was as follows:

An assault party, consisting of Dog Troop complete, under the command of Major Kirby, would cross the Maas in dinghies and mop up the enemy on Belle Isle. If possible, this part of the operation would take place in complete silence, so that the subsequent raiding and reconnaissance parties whose objective was Merum should be able to cross the island undetected.

Snow suits would be provided for everyone, whilst special sledges (already in the final stages of construction at Brigade headquarters) would enable the dinghies to be dragged over the snow from the house at De Weerd to the water's edge. Dog Troop would cross the river to Belle Isle at half-past nine on the night of the 27/28th, followed by the Merum raiding parties. The latter would return not later than seven o'clock in the morning.

If surprise was lost in the initial stages, or if Dog Troop ran into more trouble than had been originally anticipated, then heavy supporting fire from artillery, mortars, and medium machine-guns would cover their withdrawal.

4

At the appointed time the various raiding parties were assembled at the river bank, awaiting orders to proceed. The moon was clear, almost full; visibility was good—almost too good to be healthy, if we were to avoid detection.

Owing to the failure of wireless communication with the Gunners, who were waiting with their 25-pounders some miles behind us to lay down preliminary fire, the commencement of the operation was postponed nearly half an hour before the break in communication was made good.

At ten o'clock Dog Troop put out with their assault boats into the river, which was running at a speed of about six and a half knots. The Troop crossed the river success fully, despite the fact that they were nearly swept down stream by the strong current.

Meanwhile the Gunners now started to put down fire on the far side of Belle Isle, and upon Merum, 'blanketing off' the assault area in the usual fashion. Despite this diver sion, however, Dog Troop were seen by the enemy. Surprise was lost before they reached the far bank of the river, and no sooner had they landed than we, on the home bank, could hear the sounds of firing at the eastern end of the island.

And then, within a matter of minutes, the firing ceased. Major Kirby had apparently overcome opposition in his landing area, and was setting off with his Troop for the main objective—the lock area at the western end.

Ten, twenty, thirty minutes went by, and still we had no word from Dog Troop. By this time they were com pletely out of wireless touch with Colonel Gray's head quarter party on the home bank. Suddenly the vicious sounds of muffled tommy-gun fire and grenade bursts indi cated that a violent battle had broken out in the lock area. Colonel Gray immediately ordered the mortars and machine guns to fire on their prearranged targets around Belle Isle and Merum in an effort to confuse the Germans as to our real intentions. A few minutes later—it was now nearly midnight—a small party of eight Germans were seen creep ing towards Dog Troop's original landing area at the eastern end of the island, unobserved by our men who had been left behind to guard the boats. Fire was brought to bear on the enemy patrol straight away from the home bank, and all the Germans were shot up, five being killed and the remainder wounded.

The current was too swift to try and push across reinforcements to the beleaguered Dog Troop; the problem
now, in fact, was how we were to ensure adequate means
of withdrawal for them when the time came. Their situation was still confused—at least, as far as we were concerned
—and Colonel Gray ordered a small party to try and row
across the river with a length of thick rope, so that guiding
lines for the boats could be established between the two
banks.

Despite three attempts, these lines could not be ferried
over. The current was far too strong. Even with eight
men paddling, and the use of a stern oar, boats were
swept as much as four hundred yards downstream before
any sort of crossing could be achieved. Eventually, however, two boatloads of men were paddled across to reinforce
the boat guards in the landing area, and to assist in evacuating the wounded.

By this time Colonel Gray had decided to abandon the
second phase of the operation—the raid on the 'bulge'
north of Belle Isle, and the subsequent reconnaissance of
Merum. Meanwhile Dog Troop were still battling with the
Germans in the lock area, whilst in the tiny bridgehead that
had now been established by the two boatloads of reinforce
ments at the eastern end walking wounded began to come in,
to be ferried back across the icy Maas to the home bank
for medical attention.

5

The wounded came back by the boatload. They told
us that the Germans must have heard them landing at the
eastern end and laid an ambush, waiting for them to attack

the lock area. Whatever had happened, Dog Troop had been completely surprised. All the officers in the Troop were missing—one of them believed killed—and the Sergeant-Major taken prisoner, together with several other N.C.O.s and men.

The situation looked desperate. Colonel Gray ordered the Gunners and other supporting units to bring down as much fire as possible to cover the withdrawal of the raiding party. Within five minutes of the shells hammering home on the enemy area the rest of Dog Troop began to row themselves back over the river.

There was not room for them all in the boats: and so these men, some of whom had been lying in the snow for over five hours, gave up their places in the boats to the wounded survivors from Dog Troop, stripping off clothes and equipment to swim the Maas. Some of them actually swam alongside the craft, trying to help push them along. The distance between the two banks was well over one hundred yards, and the temperature several degrees below freezing point.

When they reached the home bank they were so cold they could not speak: all they could do was to gasp for breath. Colonel Gray had them evacuated immediately to De Villa, where the doctor could attend to them in the R.A.P.

Meanwhile, under cover of our supporting fire—to which the Germans were nevertheless replying with their own guns from beyond Merum—the remainder of the raiding party, together with the bulk of the wounded, were successfully withdrawn. Dog Troop had suffered a setback at the hands of the enemy: but let it be said once and for all that not one of those men returned without his rifle, Bren gun, or whatever weapon he landed with. Nothing

was abandoned to the Germans that could be used against
us.

The time was now almost four o'clock in the morning,
and the noise of battle was beginning to die down. Major
Beadle, accompanied by Captain John Griffiths (10 Commando), took a small patrol across to the island to search
for those of our wounded who were still missing, and to
secure at least one prisoner for the purposes of information.

It was five o'clock before they returned, to report that
they had found five dead Germans, including an Artillery
officer, and taken one prisoner. A map found on the body
of the dead officer proved of the greatest value, giving in
detail the positions of *Kamfgruppe* (Battle group) Hubner,
who had fought us at Brachterbeek three days before, and
also the positions of Regiment Muller, who were occupying
both Belle Isle and the Merum area.

Of our wounded there was no further sign. They were
in enemy hands, there was no doubt about that now. One
of the N.C.O.s, Sergeant Jock Fenwick, although wounded
in the leg, succeeded in making his escape, crawling alone
in the snow across the island from the lock area. He was
brought back with Ian Beadle's patrol.

At a quarter-past six we put down our last torrent of
fire on the enemy occupying the island, then set off for De
Villa, a bunch of tired, angry men.

Dawn was breaking as we reached Commando headquarters—cold, grey and forbidding, with ugly streaks of
red that looked so much like blood.

6

We did not know the full extent of our casualties until
noon that day. Then the news spread round the Commando

like wildfire. One officer and ten men killed, thirteen wounded, two officers and four men missing.

Such were the bare details. The actual names of the killed and wounded—known now to be in German hands —were not confirmed until two days later.

It was decided at this stage that, whatever the loss of dignity we might incur in German eyes, we should make every possible attempt to recover our dead and wounded from Belle Isle. Accordingly, that very afternoon a small party under Captain Griffiths and Sergeant-Major Howarth (also of 10 Commando) set out for the river bank bearing a flag of truce.

Sergeant-Major Howarth, who spoke fluent German, set the flag up on the bank, then shouted to the Germans to hand us back our wounded and surrender the dead. Minutes passed before he received an answer, which was finally supplied by a young cadet officer, who emerged from a slit trench carrying a white flag. He told Howarth to come back on the following morning, when he would give the answer of his commander, Hauptmann Muller.

At nine o'clock on the 29th Howarth, Captain Griffiths and the remainder of the party went down to the river's edge again. The cadet officer again came forward with his white flag, bearing Muller's answer. We could have our dead, but not the wounded.

The grisly business of ferrying the corpses across the Maas by boat lasted the entire morning. Most of them were unrecognisable, due to exposure in the snow, and one of the last to be brought across could only be identified by two tattered cloth pips on the shoulders, and a pair of faded parachutist's wings on the right arm.

It was the body of Peter Winston.

7

The full story of that abortive raid on Belle Isle now began to come to light. Major Kirby, together with Jack Alvey—his other subaltern—and four men had been captured ; Peter Winston and ten others (previously reported missing) had been killed ; thirteen had been wounded.

All of us were angry rather than anything else. Angry to think that so many good men had been lost for nothing, and at our failure to reduce the infantry of Regiment Muller on Belle Isle. That the latter had fought bravely and behaved gallantly could not be denied: but the handing-over of a few bodies for burial was small recompense .

The truce continued for another twenty-four hours, during which time both Captain Griffiths and Sergeant-Major Howarth tried very hard to convince the German cadet officer that it would be better to surrender whilst there was still a chance of coming out of the war alive. The young German replied, however, that much as he and his comrades would like to go to England as prisoners of war, neither their honour nor Hauptmann Muller would permit them to do so.

By midnight on January 31 the truce had ended. We were again at war with Number 10 Company, Regiment Muller, on Belle Isle.

CHAPTER 10

PERIOD JANUARY 29—MARCH 22, 1945

DURING the truce period the enemy in the Merum area had brought up a nebelwerfer*, which they had used to some effect on Able Troop's positions in Linne and Commando headquarters at De Villa. Whilst we had been doing all we could for our dead and wounded on Belle Isle we had ignored this latest enemy device; but once the truce was over Colonel Gray resumed the fight. Counter-fire was brought to bear at frequent intervals on Merum, and daylight standing patrols sent down to the river bank in snow-suits, carefully watching the enemy's movements.

The Germans on Belle Isle, however, possibly thinking that we would not bother them after our fruitless raid, did not take much trouble to conceal themselves. In any case, they knew, as well as ourselves, that they were beyond effective Bren gun and rifle range.

After two days' observation by our standing patrols Colonel Gray decided that he had secured sufficient information regarding the enemy's daily habits to teach them a thorough, bitter lesson. On February 3 a troop of tanks— ' borrowed ' from the Seventh Armoured Division—rumbled down to river bank, forming up in line abreast before opening fire.

* A six-barrelled multi-mortar.

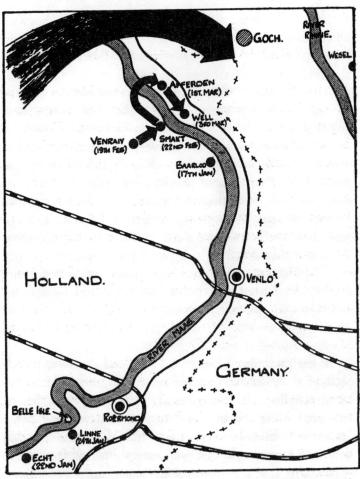

Map showing First Commando Brigade's movements in Holland, period
January 22-March 3, 1945

For some inexplicable reason the Germans ignored the tanks' presence. There was no sudden whine of mortar bombs, no screech of shells, no vicious burst of Spandaus. Perhaps they were all in their slit trenches. Anyway, wherever they were, and whatever they were doing, it certainly made things all the easier for us. Everyone was able to stand up in full view of the enemy on the river bank, and point out, in comparative ease and comfort, all the known German positions in the lock area to the tank gunners.

Those gunners did their job very efficiently. Within a matter of minutes the lock area on the island had been subjected to a most intense bombardment: but the men of Regiment Muller offered not the slightest resistance. Perhaps this surprise battering of their positions had so unnerved them that they were too frightened to do anything. Whatever their reaction during that most unpleasant twenty minutes which the tanks gave them, their future movements on the island were both greatly restricted and highly concealed, to say the least.

2

In the meantime Number 6 Commando, who were still occupying the railway station on the southern tip of the Montforterbeek, had been busily conducting a series of armoured sweeps on the ' Siegfried switch,' working in co-operation with tanks from the 8th Hussars and the 5th R.T.R. These patrols took place over the period January 26 —February 1, and an immense amount of information concerning the general defence lay-out of the ' Siegfried switch ' was obtained as a result of them.

By the first week in February, however, the thaw had begun to set in, seriously hampering movement, either by tanks or infantry. The countryside was covered with a thick slush of melting snow and slippery mud. In some parts the area was under flood, for the waters of the Maas had swollen perilously during the past week or so, finally bursting their banks to overrun a considerable portion of Belle Isle on the enemy side, and of the De Weerd area on our own. On February 7 our tanks had a last crack at the island defences, and although two of them became bogged in the process the shooting-up was highly successful. Again, the Germans made no attempt to reply.

The flooding greatly restricted operations on both sides, with the result that static warfare now became the order of the day, with the usual exchange of mortar bombs and shells. We appeared to have the initiative in this respect, for with every shell or bomb the Germans put down on us we replied threefold.

By February 13 the flooding of the De Weerd area had become so bad that Colonel Gray was obliged to withdraw Baker and Easy Troops from this outlying position, otherwise they would have been completely isolated from Commando headquarters at De Villa by a large stretch of water which had flooded the only road leading to their house.

The two Troops were accordingly withdrawn to De Villa, Commando headquarters moving to billets in the Windmill area, a few hundred yards south. The Commando defence lay-out was now as follows: Able Troop remained in the north-western tip of Linne ; Baker, Charlie and Dog Troops were on the De Villa-Linne road ; Easy Troop was now in the original Commando headquarters at De Villa, whilst the Heavy Weapons Troop of mortars and machine-guns moved into the railway station, 6 Commando having moved further south to relieve a battalion of the Devons from the line.

3

To the south of the station area the enemy now became most active and cunning with their patrolling tactics. Both 6 Commando and ourselves had numerous clashes at night with small patrols—often led by trained Alsatian dogs—which attempted to infiltrate through our lines, inflict as many casualties as possible, then withdraw speedily and silently to their own lines. These patrols were beaten off every time, however, 6 Commando having particular success upon one occasion.

It was a mid-February night, and there was little moonlight. The German patrol, believed to have consisted of about four men, led by an officer, infiltrated right into 6 Commando's positions. One of the Commando's men—a mortarman—was lying asleep at the bottom of his slit trench. Some sixth sense told him that danger was near at hand and he suddenly awoke, to observe a brawny figure peering down at him, Schmeisser* in hand.

He lay perfectly still, and the figure moved on, evidently satisfied that there was no one there. Meanwhile the mortarman calmly reached for his pistol, and rose to his feet. As he peered over the top of his trench he saw the backs of the enemy patrol facing him, about five yards away. He immediately shot two of them dead through the back, whilst his comrades despatched the rest.

This incident soon went the rounds in the Brigade, and it wasn't long before some wag made up a highly indecent rhyme entitled " *Dan, Dan, the Mortarman. . . .*"

A few nights later a large patrol from our own Commando set out from the station area to try and ascertain

*German sub-machine-gun.

whether or not the Germans were holding the forward edge of Heide Wood. This wood lay approximately four hundred yards south-east of the station.

The patrol itself was not highly successful, for no signs of the Germans were found at all on the edge of the wood, although it was known that they were occupying it in strength in some parts. By six o'clock in the morning our men were back in their billets at the station, having returned through our lines by a very circuitous route so as to avoid being followed.

About twenty minutes later a German patrol came along the road leading to the station. One of our men, who was on guard in a slit trench saw them coming, and immediately trained his Bren gun on them, purely as a precautionary measure.

He waited until the patrol was almost on top of him, then softly murmured for them to halt and give the pass-word. Immediately the leader of the German patrol hissed, "Shut up, or we'll kill you," in perfect English. Then the entire patrol threw themselves upon him.

Fortunately for us, the Germans had picked the wrong man to have a scrap with. This particular Marine weighed about fourteen stone, and was an accomplished boxer. Single-handed, he engaged them all, and there was a furious set-to, lasting some three minutes. In the meantime the warning had been given to the rest of us inside the nearby houses, for the noise of the scuffle was far from slight, with a burly young Marine yelling for help at the top of his voice.

We rushed outside to see what was happening: but by the time we had done so the Germans had finally succeeded in lifting the Marine out of the trench, and were now busy carrying him bodily up the road. We daren't open fire for fear of hitting him, and so started to give chase.

The enemy panicked immediately. Dropping the now half-conscious Marine in the road they fled for safety, but not before one of their number had discharged a Panzer-faust* at the door of one of the houses, slightly wounding a sergeant.

Although we chased them for a good half-mile up the road we could not catch them. They vanished into the darkness, completely and utterly.

We later learned that the German troops carrying out this patrolling—they formed part of none other than Battle Group Hubner—had been organised into a special patrolling section, consisting of forty picked men, most of whom spoke excellent English. Led by dogs, their sole duties were to patrol into our lines and cause as much trouble as possible.

4

After this incident Coloney Gray decided to strengthen our position in the station area, whereupon Baker, Charlie and Dog Troops were moved from the De Villa-Linne road, to come under the direct command of Major de Courcy-Ireland, who had set up a subsidiary headquarters there.

The situation on our left flank had become extremely quiet in the meantime, and although we still continued to observe all enemy movement on Belle Isle we nevertheless felt that Regiment Muller—unlike their friends in Heide Wood—were far from aggressive, especially as their island was still under partial flood. However, should they decide to attack De Villa, we still had Able and Easy Troops on that flank to deal with them.

---

* This was a long, tubular weapon fitted with a warhead at one end. Its real use in the German Army was as an anti-tank weapon—the equivalent of the British PIAT—but the German infantry, however, frequently used it as a personal weapon, as did British troops later on in the campaign, when discarded Panzerfausts were plentiful.

On February 16 orders came from Brigade headquarters to the effect that an American battalion would be taking over our sector, and that the entire Brigade would shortly be moving north. Apparently the Allied Armies were carrying out regrouping on a large scale, for the British and Canadian forces were being concentrated in the northern half of the Allied line, with the Americans in the southern half.

We decided to give Battle Group Hubner one final hammering before we departed. The whole of the morning of the 16th was devoted to Heide Wood, which was heavily engaged with mortar and medium machine-gun fire. In the afternoon we turned our attentions to the now inoffensive gentlemen of Regiment Muller residing on Belle Isle. A small patrol under Ian Beadle took a medium machine-gun and a K gun down to the river bank—the floods having decreased a little by this time—and opened fire across the water for the last time. Ironically enough, Hauptmann Muller's men replied on this occasion with a most vigorous fusilade of rifle, Spandau and mortar fire. Fortunately, however, Ian Beadle withdrew his patrol without sustaining any casualties.

Three days later, on February 19, an American infantry battalion arrived to take over. Masses of guns and vehicles drew up in convoy, completely blocking the road running from Chap to the Windmill. This, we were told by a red-faced American captain, was just the normal U.S. Army set-up. We admired the quality of such equipment, but did not stay to either argue or advise as to how such enormous quantities of it were to be suitably dispersed in so small an area. We had to be moving. Our destination was many miles north.

5

It was drizzling with rain when we reached Venray, a tiny Dutch town lying just behind the Maas. All of us were soaked to the skin as we drove through the almost deserted streets, for we had been riding in open trucks for over seven hours.

No sooner had we de-bussed than Brigadier Mills-Roberts ordered us into reserve, whilst the remaining units of the Brigade moved up into the line, on the banks of the Maas —a sector, incidentally, which was on the extreme left of the British Army.

The German troops opposite us were extremely quiet, despite the fact that our Intelligence officers had discovered that Battle Group Hubner had moved north from the Roermond area on almost the same day as we had, and were now known to be somewhere in the immediate vicinity.

Meanwhile, a few miles further north, troops of the First Canadian Army were conducting a determined drive south of the town of Goch—now reduced to a heap of rubble after a vicious series of battles through the dense Reichswald Forest. This they were doing in an effort to trap the bulk of the German Army between the Maas and the Rhine.

On February 22 we were ordered up into the line, and accordingly left our comfortable billets in Venray, where the local Dutch people had been very kind to us, to occupy the nearby village of Smakt, which was on the left of the Brigade positions.

For the next five days very little happened, apart from the usual shelling and mortaring, which both sides appeared to be indulging in in the most perfunctory fashion, adhering rigidly to the customs and traditions of static warfare. On the 28th, 3 Commando relieved us, and we accordingly moved back to Venray again. No one—except, possibly, Colonel Gray—quite knew why we were going back into reserve after only six days in the line. The rumour-mongers concluded that something was definitely ' on.'

For once, they were right. The Canadian drive in the north had gone well. Driven steadily southwards, the Germans were now threatened with complete annihilation by the advancing Canadians to their front, and by Second British Army on their flank. Our Brigade was now split into two halves. Numbers 6 and 45 Commandos, together with Brigade headquarters, were placed under command of 52nd (Lowland) Division, whilst 3 and 46 Commandos remained in their positions on the Maas to form ' Grayforce,' named after the Commanding Officer of 46, Lieutenant-Colonel T. M. Gray, D.S.O., R.M., who had been placed in charge.

Under command of 52 Division 6 Commando and ourselves were under orders to follow up the Canadian drive between the two rivers. Accordingly, at eight o'clock on the following morning, March 1, we moved by transport to Afferden, a small, recently captured village on the east bank of the Maas. On arrival we de-bussed, to receive further orders to the effect that we were to relieve the Reconnaissance elements of 52 Division as soon as it was dark. They were at present some miles to the south, in the van of the drive on the retreating enemy.

We made ourselves as comfortable as we could in our billets, and waited for the order to move. Tea-time and twilight, supper-time and darkness, all came and went: but still we received no orders. Perhaps, we thought, they weren't going to need us after all.

The following morning, news was heard of the Reconnaissance forces. During the night they had received orders to attack certain German positions south of Afferden,

and having moved forward under cover of darkness, had
attacked at dawn. The subsequent battle was still being
waged, and it looked very much as if the enemy defences
would be overrun.

It was not until the evening that we were finally ordered
to relieve the men of the Reconnaissance Regiment. Even
then the position was very confused, for the Germans had
apparently succeeded in holding out against all attacks in a
concrete factory on the extreme right, overlooking the Maas.
However, with great difficulty the change-over between the
two units was eventually effected, and the Reconnaissance
Regiment accordingly withdrew to Afferden, leaving us to
hold the newly captured territory.

That night, in pitch blackness, we silently dug ourselves
in. The ground was very soft, being composed of sand
dunes, so it was not very long before everyone was well
and truly ' underground.' There was no activity during the
night, which was just as well, for we had not the slightest
idea of the whereabouts of any other British units, and had
there been any friendly patrols out we should have been
none the wiser, and might have accidentally shot them up in
consequence.

6

The dawn broke, warm and sunny, with the whole unit
' standing-to ' in their slit trenches. There was nothing
to be seen of the enemy for miles around. The whole of the
countryside consisted of flat, barren sand dunes which
stretched with weary monotony for miles southwards.

At half-past eight we received further orders from Divisional headquarters. Supported by a squadron of tanks we
were to advance as rapidly as possible down the east bank of

the Maas until we made contact with the enemy—if there was any enemy left to contact and fight.

Throughout the day we moved at speed, alternating between marching on foot and riding on the backs of the tanks. We did not halt until six o'clock in the evening, on the outskirts of the town of Bergen, where we had a hasty meal. An hour later we resumed our march, led by Ian Beadle. This proved to be an extremely lengthy and tedious night infiltration, which was totally uneventful, for there were no Germans about. The only things we had to be careful about—and we looked for them literally every yard of the way—were mines.

Late that night we finally reached Well, a town seven miles south of Bergen. Once again there were no enemy to be seen. We rested for the night, and on the following morning sent a patrol across the Maas to 'Grayforce' for rations.

It seemed obvious now that the bulk of the German forces had retreated across the Rhine. The few stragglers we had 'winkled out' from various German trenches confirmed this theory. Meanwhile, as we could expect no transport down the eastern side of the river for at least forty-eight hours, we had to rely on 'Grayforce' for daily rations and supplies. For almost a week, from March 4-10, we remained in Well, resting.

7

Ahead of us lay Germany. Soon we would be crossing the Rhine: but there was every indication of a lull before we did so, and with this knowledge we made ourselves as comfortable as possible in the meantime.

The honour of being the first Commando troops to enter the Third Reich fell to a fighting Troop of 46 Commando. These men crossed the Maas, moved through Well—where we were still resting—and penetrated as far east as the village of Walbeck, which was some miles beyond the German border. No enemy troops were encountered, and the patrol returned after having made contact with reconnaissance elements of the American Army, who had patrolled up from the south.

We were at the gateway to Germany. The final advance was near at hand.

PART THREE

GERMANY

CHAPTER 11

PERIOD MARCH 10—MARCH 23, 1945

ON March 10 we moved back to Venray, where training
for the Rhine crossing began in earnest. The Maas itself
became the rehearsal area for the proposed operation, and
although the actual plan for the assault was not divulged
to us until we had moved up to the marshalling area on the
banks of the Rhine on the 19th, most of us had a very fair
idea of what was expected of us.

The entire Brigade commenced ' refresher ' training on
water. At first ordinary Goatleys—small collapsible
dinghies—were used to practise with, but later Buffaloes*
were used, and everyone wore full equipment, as they would
when the operation came off. In fact, towards the end of
our training we trained with Buffaloes both day and night,
learning how to embark and disembark from them as quickly
as possible.

Although priority was given to this water training,
we also put in a little extra practice in weapon training and
street fighting. This was to prove invaluable later on.

On the evening of March 19, transport arrived in Venray to move us to the marshalling area. We embussed in the
trucks and for four hours moved at a steady, monotonous
speed towards the Rhine. We passed through the town
of Venlo, then over the German border, until we finally

* Armoured amphibious troop carriers.

reached our destination—a bone factory some two miles west of the Rhine, opposite the town of Wesel, Hitler's much-vaunted 'bastion of the Ruhr.' It was bitterly cold that night, and drizzling with rain. In dead silence we all de-bussed from the trucks and made our way to our allotted billets in the darkness.

2

We spent three days in the marshalling area, during which time our activities consisted solely of checking and re-checking our equipment, resting as much as possible, and going over and over the plan for the assault crossing.

Apart from this we also had ample time to observe the colossal preparations which 21st Army Group were making for this 'last great heave,' as Mr. Churchill had termed it. Everywhere, as far as the eye could see, were masses of tanks, guns and supplies of every description, with literally thousands of troops encamped on the banks of the Rhine. On every main road leading up to the various divisional marshalling areas there was a never-ending stream of convoys, bringing up even more men and equipment. To hide all this activity from the watchful Germans on the eastern bank of the river, 21st Army Group were in the process of putting up a thick, continuous smoke-screen from thousands of canisters of chemicals lying, neatly stacked in piles, along the road running parallel to the Rhine itself. This smoke-screen doubtless denied the enemy the chance of observing much that was going on, but nevertheless it made us all feel extremely sick when the wind blew the wrong way.

For us, now, the all-important matter was the plan, which everyone in the Brigade had to know, from Brigadier Mills-Roberts downwards. Briefly, it was as follows:

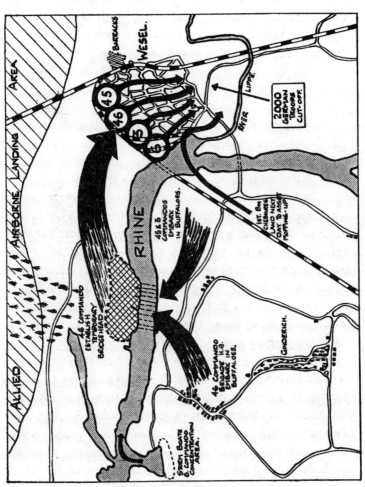

Crossing the Rhine. First Commando Brigade's assault on Wesel

In mounting ' Operation Plunder,' as the Rhine crossing was called, 21st Army Group had allotted a special task to First Commando Brigade—the seizure and holding of the town of Wesel. This subsidiary operation was known as ' Operation Widgeon.'

The entire success of the Rhine crossing depended, to a very great extent, on ' Widgeon.' It was known that there was a large number of troops in Wesel—conservative estimates were in the region of 2,000—and if we could successfully surprise and hold this force, then the success of crossings at other points of the Rhine by units of the 15th (Scottish) and 51st (Highland) Divisions would be assured.

Brigadier Mills-Roberts' plan was this. On the night of March 23 (R minus One), at ten o'clock, 46 Commando, under Lieutenant-Colonel T. M. Gray, would cross the Rhine in Buffaloes and land at the basin of low-lying, marshy ground known as Grav Insel, which lay about two miles downstream from Wesel. From this point they would proceed four hundred yards inland to hold a small beach-head, whilst the remainder of the Brigade came ashore in successive waves of craft. The order of landing would thus be 46 Commando, followed by 6, 45, Brigade headquarters, and 3 Commandos.

To divert the enemy's attention whilst the landing was in progress, and to deceive them as to our actual embarkation point from the western bank, 6 Commando were to make the crossing in small, noisy storm-boats, assembling in a large creek just over a mile downstream from the Brigade's main embarkation area.

In addition to this the Brigade were to receive tremendous fire support whilst the landing was in progress. Allotted to us by 8 Corps—under whose direct command we had been placed for the operation—for ' softening up ' known

German positions on the Grav Insel sector were three Super Heavy batteries of artillery, together with one heavy gun regiment, seven medium artillery regiments, ten Field regiments (25-pounders), one heavy ack-ack regiment, and numerous detachments of 4.2 and 3-inch mortars.

After the beach-head had been successfully established by 46 Commando, and the rest of the Brigade landed, the second phase of 'Widgeon' would commence. This consisted of a Brigade advance in single file—'snake'—across the three thousand yards of flat, open ground lying between Grav Insel and Wesel, to be followed by an assault on Wesel itself. 6 Commando, having landed immediately behind 46, were to advance with all speed at the head of the Brigade column into Wesel and seize a bridgehead in the northern tip of the town. Once this had been achieved 45 Commando, following up straight away, would move into their objective —a wire factory just beyond 6 Commando's area. In similar fashion 3 and 46 Commandos would follow suit, the latter being the last to leave the temporary beach-head.

Deadline for the final positions to be occupied in Wesel was daybreak on the 24th. If this was successfully accomplished, then some two thousand German infantry of all types would be trapped in the town, with no possible means of escape. The Brigade's task then would be to hold the town—and its occupants—until approximately eleven o'clock on the morning of R Day (March 24), when a combined force of British and American airborne formations would drop to the east of Wesel and join forces with us.

Such was the plan ; and basically, it was a simple one. We had ample support—the R.A.F. had agreed to bomb Wesel into the bargain, weather permitting—and so all that was required from us was speed, and determination. We had, after landing, to reach Wesel and secure those positions by daybreak. If the Germans caught us at night in low-lying Grav Insel we should probably be annihilated.

3

The sun blazed down on the seemingly placid waters of the Rhine on the morning of Friday, March 23. Just behind the ever-present smoke-screen Lieutenant-General Ritchie, the Commander of 8 Corps, was speaking to a huddled group of men that was our Commando. He told us that we were going to cross the Rhine that night.

' I think,' he said, ' although my knowledge of military history is a little rusty, that you will be the first British troops ever to have crossed this river. Not even Marlborough attempted it.'

Brigadier Mills-Roberts also addressed us that morning. His words were full of fire and zeal, and whipped us all into a frenzy of enthusiasm for the assault. He repeated the plan, he numbered the guns, the mortars, and other supporting weapons that were to support us. He told us where, when and how and the R.A.F. would be helping us, and what the Airborne troops would do on the following day. He had all the intricate details of ' Widgeon ' to his finger-tips, and never once had to consult any notes. Finally, amidst cheers, he said: ' . . . Never in the history of human warfare have so many guns supported so few men. When you go in tonight, cut hell out of them ! '

We were supposed to rest for the remainder of the day: but most of us just couldn't now. All we could do was wait patiently, talk about the operation, check our weapons and ammunition. We were too excited to eat. . . .

At seven o'clock that night, three hours before H Hour, the whole of our Brigade was formed up on the western bank of the Rhine. Everyone lay about in scattered groups, their faces blackened, green berets on their heads—we never wore tin helmets—and laden with assault equipment.

During those last hours before we went over rum and biscuits were served out, together with the mail, which we all tried very hard to read in the darkness, by the light of carefully concealed candles and hurricane lamps. Meanwhile, the Buffaloes began to arrive on the road leading towards the river.

At eight o'clock the Gunners opened up their ' softening programme ' on Grav Insel. Within the space of seconds the air was filled with the angry rumble of heavy guns, the thunderous roar of nearby 25-pounder Regiments, the pop-popping of hundreds of mortars, and the insistent chatter of Vickers machine-guns.

A few hundred yards in front of us the slim ribbon that was the Rhine became almost hidden with the reddish bursts of thousands of shells, each of which left thick, weaving clouds of smoke. Away to the right, around Wesel, it seemed as if thousands of candles had been lighted and sus-pended like so many fairy lights over the town as orange-coloured tracer shells from light anti-aircraft guns curved in a series of graceful parabola towards their targets. The dull night sky gleamed strangely with a ruddy glow as fires were started.

Whilst all this was going on, a B.B.C. commentator —who shall be nameless—was wandering around the Buffa-loes, talking to our men and asking them various questions, microphone in hand. From one young North Country Marine to whom he put the rather ridiculous question, ' Do you think you'll be first across ? ' the answer came pat enough : ' Not if I can bloody well help it, mate.'

After that, the B.B.C. man completely disappeared.

4

For the next two hours the Gunners continued to blast away at their targets. At ten minutes to ten the Buffaloes started to warm into life, and as their engines thundered into a roar which seemed to drown the noise of the gunfire, everyone hoped that they wouldn't be heard by the enemy, now little more than a mile away.

The entire Brigade was soon embarked in the Buffaloes, the faint moonlight gleaming in ghostly fashion upon their bodies and equipment, picking out the shoulders of a man here, the snub nose of a tommy-gun there, as they crouched in the wells of their craft.

With a steadily increasing roar, followed by a sharp jerk, the first wave of four Buffaloes suddenly leaped forward and raced to the water's edge. The gunfire was as loud as ever, and the whole fury of our supporting weapons continued unabated.

The Buffaloes reached the bottom of the massive dyke which lay between them and the Rhine, then climbed slowly, laboriously, over the top, to slide down the other side and enter the water with a thunderous splash. Meanwhile the Gunners began to concentrate their fire on the landing bays, standing by to lift their barrage ten yards inland the moment the Buffaloes touched down on the enemy bank.

As the first wave of 46 Commando jumped out of their craft to wade ashore a new sound could be heard, very faintly at first, high above the roar of successive explosions. It was the heartening drone of R.A.F. Lancaster bombers. They were still some way off, and it would probably be twenty to twenty-five minutes before they arrived over Wesel. Meanwhile the remainder of the Brigade, headed by the other Troops of 46, were pouring across the river.

6 Commando's storm-boats could be clearly heard as they issued forth from the creek downstream, despite the fact that the Germans seemed to be shelling their area more consistently than anywhere else. They probably thought that the entire Brigade was embarking there, which was precisely what we wanted them to think.

Together with 3 Commando we formed the last waves to cross the river. The operation was going just like clockwork ; and as we touched down, wave after wave of us, at Grav Insel we could see, in the light of a furiously blazing Buffalo which had been hit by a chance shell, the first prisoners coming in from the perimeter of 46 Commando's beach-head. They all seemed utterly dazed with the shelling, with absolutely no fight in them.

Punctually at half-past ten the Lancasters arrived over their target. Two hundred and fifty bombers reduced Wesel, within the short space of fifteen minutes, to rubble and burning embers. As the last aircraft wheeled and droned away back to its base in England, 6 Commando entered the town, followed by the rest of us.

By one o'clock in the morning the entire Brigade had reached the centre of Wesel, and was busy trying to find its various defensive areas, as originally planned. Maps were useless at this juncture, for the town now consisted of a series of enormous craters, surrounded by the shells of bomb-blasted buildings. There were literally no roads, and very few of the side streets had been left intact. The railway—formerly a first-class landmark—had been reduced to a series of broken pieces of line, straggling in rather ungainly fashion through the rubble. Nearly every building left standing was burning.

The R.A.F. had certainly done a good job. To cap it all, there were thousands of German troops known to be at large somewhere in Wesel. Probably most of them were skulking in deep cellars by this time, like all the civilians who had remained in the town.

We advanced in single file along both sides of a main street running north, which we hoped would bring us to our final positions. There were a lot of supposedly dead Germans lying about here, and just as Colonel Gray and his headquarters party neared the corner of the street to turn north for the wire factory—our final position—a ' dead ' German (we later identified him as belonging to the S.S.) suddenly rose to his feet and fired a Panzerfaust at point-blank range. The result of this sudden onslaught was that two of the headquarters men were killed, Colonel Gray wounded in the arm, and nearly everyone in the immediate vicinity knocked off their feet by the force of the explosion.

Feeling very angry we emptied a magazine of tommy-gun bullets into the German soldier, and into every subsequent ' corpse ' we saw lying around. That S.S. man had taught us a very bitter lesson.

5

There was no more fighting that night. We reached the wire factory at approximately two o'clock in the morning and found, to our great surprise, that it wasn't a wire factory at all, but one engaged solely in the manufacture of lavatory pans. As soon as we got inside the factory we set to work feverishly to barricade it as much as possible. Machinery, timber, doors, benches, coils of wire—all were used in an effort to prepare rough defensive positions, blocking windows and the like until they were mere loopholes. Elsewhere in the Brigade very much the same sort of thing was going on, and throughout the night we waited for an enemy counter-attack which never came.

When dawn broke the next morning Easy Troop were ' standing to ' in their positions, which lay in the right-hand corner of the factory, facing east. There was still nothing happening: it seemed, in fact, as if all would be quiet, and that the Airborne troops would have nothing at all to worry about when they dropped at eleven o'clock.

Suddenly a Marine, looking out his loophole, saw a dozen rather weary German soldiers wheeling cycles down the road leading back into the town. They were heading straight for the factory. Everyone in the Troop waited for them to come closer, their weapons at the ready.

The Germans obviously thought that, wherever the British were, they were certainly not in the lavatory-pan factory. They chatted amongst themselves quite unsus-pectingly as they came towards the men of Easy Troop, all of whom were now on aim, awaiting the order to open fire.

A few minutes later the Germans passed within a few feet of Easy Troop: but the latter still held their fire. Then, as the last German presented his back to them, the Troop opened up. Thirty seconds later there were twelve corpses in the road.

So far this had been our only brush with the enemy. It was not until about nine o'clock that they put in their first organised counter-attack; and when it came it seemed to be a most half-hearted affair, consisting of a few ragged waves of infantry, supported by cumbersome Mark IV tanks and self-propelled guns. The infantry were easily beaten off, and for some unknown reason the tanks did not attempt to come too close. Had they done so, of course, they would have caused untold damage, for our defensive posi-tions were far from perfect, and we had nothing more than

L

PIATs and a Panzerfaust or two with which to defend ourselves against armour.

There were, in fact, only two real attempts by German
tanks to dislodge us. The first was when a solitary Mark IV,
braver than its fellows, started to rumble ominously down
the main road towards us. It got to within one hundred
and fifty yards of the factory, then became indecisive. Major
Beadle, meanwhile, had mustered every available PIAT and
Panzerfaust, and these were on aim, waiting to fire.

Suddenly the tank stopped altogether, its engines coughing and arguing, then turned round, heading back the way it
came. Discretion being the better part of valour, Easy
Troop let it go.

About half an hour later—the time was now just after
ten o'clock—a second Mark IV approached to within 250
yards of the factory, and commenced to pump shells into it.
As it was out of PIAT range and our artillery had been for-
bidden to open fire owing to the fact that the Airborne
landings were imminent, there was really nothing to be done
about it : so we just lay quietly under what cover we could,
enduring a most unpleasant bombardment of 75-millimetre
shells, until the German crew in the Mark IV finally tired
of their party games, and withdrew.

Whilst all this had been going on, a fighting Troop of
46 Commando, who were in a builder's yard on the far side
of the road opposite us, had been conducting a small war
of their own against scattered parties of Germans who were
scurrying about isolated buildings in a small village three
hundred yards to the east of the town. They had been sniping at them throughout the morning with devastating
accuracy, and there was no doubt at all that this largely con-
tributed to the enemy's failure to mount any really large-
scale attack. Every time they brought up an SP gun, or their

infantry formed up in the village buildings for a possible advance, they were fired upon. 46 Commando inflicted a lot of casualties in this manner.

Elsewhere the Brigade had been holding their own quite successfully. Both 3 and 6 Commandos had been sniping throughout the morning as well, whilst Brigade headquarters had succeeded in killing a German general (Deutsche by name), who wanted to shoot matters out from the cellar in which he was hiding, together with his staff. The latter surrendered after their leader had been despatched by a Commando sergeant-major armed with a tommy-gun.

7

At eleven o'clock that morning, dead on time, the Airborne troops came in. The sunny sky was filled with the drone of hundreds of aircraft, which we couldn't see at first, but which were eventually identified as hosts of Liberators and Dakotas, flying in from the north in rigid formation, about a mile east of Wesel.

It was a wonderful sight: we could not help cheering, despite the fact that, somewhere well out of our range, the Germans were putting up an intense barrage of ack-ack fire. Nevertheless, those planes never wavered for a single instant in their course. On and on they came, until they were right over the target. The gliders calmly banked to find their landing zones, whilst amidst the tiny puffs of ack-ack fire in the distance, we could see thousands of white patches twisting and swaying in the sky, each patch a man, and no bigger than a thimble from where we were.

These were the men we had been waiting for—the men of the British Sixth Airborne Division and the American Eighteenth Airborne Corps. We were very glad to see them, particularly the former, with whom we remembered a somewhat similar meeting beyond the River Orne, in Normandy a few months before.

Yes, it was great to see the men of the Sixth Airborne Division again.

CHAPTER 12

PERIOD MARCH 24—APRIL 9, 1945

THE arrival of the airborne force spelt finis for the Wermacht. Already they had been rolled back many miles east of Wesel: the town was still a twisted, ruined mass, no longer part of the front line, but an ever-growing store-house, into which stores and supplies of every sort were being poured from the home back of the Rhine.

Our engineers had succeeded in bridging the river, which meant that troops and stores no longer had to be ferried across in Buffaloes and Weasels. They were being brought over in vast columns of lorries passing through our positions in Wesel to the battle that was now flaring intermittently beyond. Tanks were beginning to come over, too. The last barrier to Germany, on which the Wermacht High Command had pinned all their hopes on making a stand, had been overcome with astounding ease.

For us, however, still in Wesel, there were one or two changes, not the least of which was the evacuation from the battle area of Colonel Gray, whose arm was giving him more trouble than John Tulloch, our doctor, could cope with. Command of the unit was assumed in Colonel Gray's absence by Major A. L. Blake, a young fair-haired veteran of the Italian campaign, who had recently joined us to replace Major de Courcy-Ireland, he having departed from the unit just after the Battle of Brachterbeek to take over a special Royal Marine unit which was at present operating in another part of the line.

Before receiving any further orders to move—and it rather looked as if we should remain in Wesel for a few days, at least—the Brigadier ordered us to rest. We made the most of this: everyone salvaged beds for themselves, Brigade headquarters brought up more rations, and we even received mail and newspapers containing accounts of our crossing of the Rhine. These Press reports were quite accurate, though highly coloured. One famous war corres- pondent had even written for his national daily—he was describing a visit to our Brigade in Wesel—'Every time I visit these men there is an atmosphere of death. . . .' As all of us immediately pointed out—what on earth did he expect? Death, at that time, was our business.

2

Meanwhile, the Sixth Airborne Division had been placed under command of 12 Corps, like ourselves. Together with the 6th Guards Armoured Brigade they made ready for a dash across the North German plain, with the city of Munster as their first objective.

We envied the men of Sixth Airborne: they had been able to arrange transport in the shape of tanks to ferry them across Germany. For our part, however, we had nothing more than our legs to move on. Our first march was merci- fully short, from Wesel to the tiny village of Dravenack, which was a distance of about ten miles. For this move— bearing in mind the fact that the remainder of Second Army had a plentiful supply of lorries—we requisitioned every- thing that could possibly be of use to help us. Cycles, prams, handcarts, captured civilian cars—all were pressed into service if it meant that they would help us forward a little faster than our own feet.

We spent the night in comfortable beds in Dravenack, marching a further twelve miles north-east on the following day, our destination this time being the village of Erle. By now, however, it had become quite obvious that our improvised transport would, in the majority of cases, have to be discarded owing to the fact that it was most unreliable, and always breaking down. The prams, cycles and so forth were accordingly ' ditched ' on arrival at Erle.

Command of our Brigade suddenly reverted from 12 to 8 Corps at this juncture. Whatever this change-over meant to Second Army headquarters, it certainly meant one good thing to us: we were given some transport. A whole company of R.A.S.C. lorries was placed at the Brigade's disposal. We all cheered for sheer joy.

Our next move was to the town of Greven, and no sooner had we billeted ourselves here than we heard that elements of the Sixth Airborne Division had crossed the Dortmund-Ems canal and reached the gates of Osnabruck, a large city exactly one hundred miles east of the Rhine.

The Brigade was ordered to pass through the Sixth Airborne Division and capture Osnabruck without delay. We accordingly prepared for battle again.

3

The ride to Osnabruck was both long and exhausting. For over nineteen hours we were in the backs of swaying bumping lorries that seemed to move all to slowly over the rough country roads. In addition to this it drizzled with rain at studied intervals.

Five miles west of Osnabruck we finally halted and

received orders to de-bus from the trucks and rest. The time
was fifteen minutes past three on the morning of April 4.

Muttering and cursing, hunting for our kit in the darkness, we jumped out of the lorries on to the roadside. All
of us were ravenously hungry, but fortunate the ' Q ' depart-
ment were on top line, and within a matter of minutes
everyone had been served out with compo rations and mugs
of steaming tea. Meanwhile, Major Blake called the Troop
Commanders together to issue his orders. The Brigade plan
was to advance into Osnabruck straight away, Number 3
Commando leading, followed by 45, 46 and 6. The town
would be entered from the high ground to the north-west
before dawn, the Brigade passing through an Airborne
Battalion's positions *en route*.

We set off at a quarter to four. The approach march
was quite uneventful, although 3 Commando clashed with a
number of small parties of the enemy on their way in. By
the time our unit arrived in Osnabruck it was evident that
the Germans were not prepared to give battle in any sort of
strength, but were merely content to restrict themselves
to sniping from windows and rooftops, and manning
' suicide ' machine-gun posts.

As is always the case, we lost a number of men during
the resultant street fighting: the actual figure was four
killed and twenty-nine wounded. By eight o'clock the
following morning, however, the city was more or less clear.

Later in the day patrols from all units in the Brigade
were sent out from their various areas in and around the
high ground, and the whole of Osnabruck was thus eventually cleared. In a matter of hours we had captured the
largest town in Germany which had so far been assaulted
by British troops, the Brigade's ' bag ' of prisoners being
somewhere in the region of 450.

Our main problem now was to stop widespread looting by the thousands of displaced persons—impressed from France, Belgium, Poland and practically every other former German-occupied country—as well as by the German citizens themselves. Down at the railway station and marshalling yards (bombed with great accuracy by the R.A.F.) a large crowd of former German slaves were merrily enjoying their first few hours of freedom. Laughing Polish girls were busy trying on fur coats, French women were looting stockings, whilst the majority of the men were hunting for food. It took us all our time to put guards on the warehouses to prevent wholesale theft, and what happened when we finally moved on and left Osnabruck unguarded could have been anybody's guess.

Some idea of the speed of our advance could be gauged from the fact that the last civilian train left Osnabruck for Berlin about five hours before we entered it.

4

On April 6 our Brigade was placed under the direct command of a division once more—none other than the celebrated Eleventh Armoured Division ; and in early morning we were moving up in company with them to a marshalling area on the western bank of the River Weser.

It was midday before we arrived at the marshalling area, where our unit was billeted in the small village of Stolzenau. Here we received news to the effect that the Weser had already been crossed by a battalion of the Rifle Brigade. Our own orders were to cross to reinforce the bridgehead they had made, and if possible, to break out of it to clear the German-held village of Leese, which lay opposite Stolzenau.

Major Blake wasted no time on receipt of these instructions from the Brigadier, and in the face of very heavy fire
from enemy artillery and 20-millimetre guns we crossed the
narrow river in assault boats. Once ashore we ran into
determined opposition, which was not altogether surprising,
despite the fact that the Rifle Brigade had preceded us, for
the particular German unit we were up against was later
identified as a training battalion of the 12th S.S. Panzer
Division.

The enemy's stand made the capture of Leese too great
a task for our Commando to undertake alone, in view of the
fact that we were outnumbered by at least three to one.
Brigadier Mills-Roberts accordingly ordered us to hold on
to the bridgehead in company with the Rifle battalion, until
the remaining Commando units could be ferried over. As
there were not sufficient boats available for this, however, it
didn't look as if we should be reinforced for some considerable time. Major Blake therefore decided to make a tentative
advance on Leese.

Meanwhile the fighting in the bridgehead had become
nothing short of desperate. The S.S. were sniping at us with
deadly accuracy, and our casualties were steadily mounting
in consequence. Able Troop, feeling their way forward
amongst the hedgerows on the edge of the bridgehead, ran
into a small party of Germans, and a furious hand-to-hand
struggle resulted. It was during this short, sharp engagement
that Captain Dudley Coventry—Able Troop's commander
—was credited with striking a German soldier dead with
one blow of his fist.

The German soldier, a young boy in the S.S., came at
Captain Coventry from behind a hedgerow. The latter, to use
his own words, was 'very annoyed' by this time, and before
the startled German could do or say anything he had felled

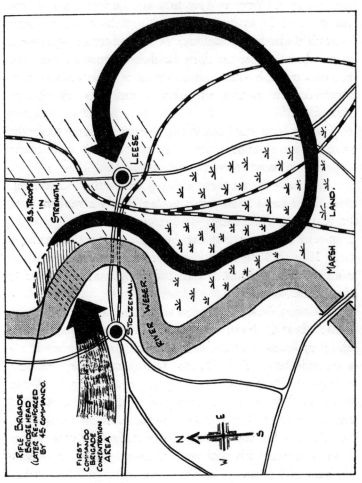

The Weser Crossing and the attack on Leese

him to the ground with one mighty blow to the jaw. When our padre reached the body some minutes later, thinking that he would have to give first aid, he found that it was lifeless. . . .

Still under heavy shellfire, we formed up in single file to make a break out of the bridgehead and commence the attack proper on Leese. The time was now four o'clock in the afternoon, and we were supposed to reach Leese by nightfall. As we steadily advanced due east upon the village, however, opposition from the fanatical S.S. troops became so intense that we were obliged to dig in about a mile short of our objective in order to hold our ground.

We held on to these fresh positions until midnight: then word came from the Brigadier that we were to withdraw to the Rifle Brigade's bridgehead, as the remaining Commando units could not be ferried over that night to support our attack. The withdrawal was accordingly carried out, every man being within the bridgehead perimeter by dawn. No sooner had the withdrawal been completed, however, than a heavy counter-attack came in from the right flank. Baker Troop, under John Day, were dug in here, and they bore the brunt of this assault almost alone. It was eventually beaten off with heavy casualties to the enemy.

5

Throughout the following day (April 7), our bridgehead was shelled with merciless intensity by enemy 88-millimetre guns. It was as much as we could do to hold on at this stage, let alone attempt a further attack on Leese. In the meantime we hoped and prayed that the boats would soon come up, so that the rest of the Brigade could cross the river and come to our aid.

Darkness fell, after a day of ceaseless bombardment, and there was still no word from Brigade headquarters. It was not until eleven o'clock that the good news finally came. The boats had arrived, said the Brigade message, and the remaining Commandos would commence crossing very shortly.

The Brigadier was as good as his word: by midnight the rest of the Brigade was over, and the full-scale attack on Leese started. 6 Commando led the way, laying a white tape in the darkness, as they had done on the Rhine. They were followed by 46 and 3, with ourselves bringing up the rear. The only people left in the bridgehead—apart from the Rifle Brigade battalion—were the mortar and Vickers machine-gun teams. It was decided that it would be best to leave them there, for their equipment was too cumbersome for a tedious night march, and they would serve a more useful purpose by strengthening the bridgehead itself.

As usual, the march was long and difficult. For hours we moved across seemingly unending miles of flat, barren countryside, broken only by occasional streams and ditches, with unpleasant patches of marshland: a long, single column of nearly two thousand men, laden with equipment, whispering curses as we stumbled on the rough ground in the darkness.

By dawn 6 Commando had reached the outskirts of Leese. The enemy appeared to be quite unaware of what was going on, and when the leading element of 6 Commando unexpectedly ran into a German 20-millimetre anti-aircraft gun post they did not have a lot of trouble in mopping it up.

The rest of us passed through the town, clearing our way down the main streets. We found little sign of the enemy, beyond a few stragglers, who told us that the bulk of the S.S. troops had withdrawn some two hours before.

This was surprising news indeed, considering the type of German soldier we had been up against for the past two days. Brigadier Mills-Roberts immediately ordered 3 Commando to give chase. The latter caught up with the enemy's rearguard forces in some woods north of Leese, where a running battle ensued: but as the latter seemed determined to run for it and offer no more fight, 3 Commando called a halt and rejoined the rest of us in Leese.

Meanwhile 46 Commando patrolled into the village of Landsberg, two miles to the north-west, only to find that the Germans had withdrawn from here also, leaving a token covering party in their wake.

The battle of the Weser had been won.

CHAPTER 13

PERIOD APRIL 10—APRIL 17, 1945

WE rested for the next twenty-four hours: and in the meantime a bridge was thrown over the Weser by the Royal Engineers, so that within a very short space of time transport was across in readiness to ferry us forward on our next move.

Technically we were still acting as flank protection to 8 Corps' axis of advance: but still this did not mean that there was a lot of fighting to do ; in fact there was hardly any. We moved from village to village, always eastward, keeping up with the main body, and called in for a river crossing or special assault as required.

It was in this fashion that we travelled to the delightful village of Armensen, which lay thirty miles due east of the Weser. Here was a peaceful spot indeed, untouched by war, with an abundance of food. Needless to say, we took especial advantage of the food position, eating as many eggs and chickens as we possibly could during our short stay.

On the following morning (April 10) we found ourselves in the trucks once more, streaming out of Armensen in convoy towards a new Brigade marshalling area, overlooking the west bank of the River Aller, which is a tributary of the Weser. We knew what was going to be asked of us before we ever arrived at our destination—another assault crossing.

From the physical point of view the Aller did not look

anything like the formidable obstacle that the Rhine or Weser had been. Whilst the latter both measured hundreds of yards in breadth, and were comparatively fast-flowing, the Aller was a bare fifty yards, with a slow, sluggish current. The country on the far side was thickly wooded, with dense undergrowth, but Intelligence reports stated that the enemy's defences there were weak, consisting of not more than two infantry companies, both of them under strength.

The Brigade plan for the proposed crossing closely followed the previous method of night infiltration in single file, a white tape being laid by the leading element. The only difference on this occasion was that we hoped to rush the railway bridge at Schwarmstedt, lying about half a mile north of the road bridge. This latter bridge would thus eventually be attacked from the rear once we had gained the woods on the enemy side of the river. However, the village of Essel—on our own side—was still held by the Germans at this stage, whilst the Eleventh Armoured Division was some miles in our rear. Any direct assault on the road bridge, therefore, would mean that it would be blown by the enemy as soon as they realised our intentions. It was for this reason that Brigadier Mills-Roberts decided to pass us over the railway bridge, in the hope of achieving complete surprise.

We set off that night as soon as it was dark, with Number 3 Commando leading. At the time we did not know it, but the battle of the Aller Woods was going to be the bitterest and bloodiest in the whole of our fighting experience.

2

Before we had even started to move towards the railway

bridge at Schwarmstedt, a lot of us had had grave misgivings as to whether the enemy in Essel would have heard our approach.

Unfortunately, they did. 3 Commando had not got within two hundred yards of the railway bridge before there was a terrific explosion, and the first span slowly twisted into the river, finally coming to rest on a flat piece of marshland. However, we found that only half the charges laid by the Germans had actually detonated, and thus we were able to scramble across the wreckage to reach the far bank of the river. Meanwhile the leading element of 3 Commando had encountered a small party of German guards on the bridge itself. These were rushed, and silently despatched with fighting knives. A small bridgehead was then quickly formed and the remainder of 3 Commando, followed by ourselves, passed through to the woods beyond.

Although the bridge had been a metal one, and the noise of hundreds of hobnailed boots scrambling across it had rather worried us at the time, the Germans in the Aller Woods seemed unaware of our approach. By half-past five in the morning, in fact, the entire Brigade had penetrated the outskirts of the woods without meeting the slightest opposition, and were busily digging-in in their various unit areas. Our particular area was a slight knoll in the centre of the woods, about one thousand yards due east of the railway bridge.

For the next two and a half hours we continued to dig defensive positions, and no counter-attack came in from the enemy, whom we could see quite clearly a few hundred yards away from us, going about their early morning task of cooking, washing, shaving and so forth.

The long-awaited German reply to our infiltration into the woods finally came at eight o'clock. The attack was

M

directed—doubtless more by luck than judgment—against the positions occupied by 3 Commando and Brigade head-quarters. Brigadier Mills-Roberts immediately ordered 46 Commando (whose area was in rear of 3, on the opposite side of the main road, running due north through the woods) to launch an attack against the road bridge, which seemed to be the point from where the enemy were counter-attacking.

No sooner had the Brigadier's orders been received than 46 Commando were themselves attacked by a second wave of German infantry, coming in from the opposite direction. Whilst they fought desperately to stave off this new assault Brigadier Mills-Roberts switched 6 Commando to the role of stemming the German attack on Brigade headquarters from the bridge.

6 Commando accordingly went in, and by half-past eleven that morning had reached the bridge, only to find it blown. They therefore decided to consolidate on their newly captured ground, and whilst they were doing so the enemy launched a third counter-attack, straight at them.

The subsequent fighting was most bloody and confused. Brigade headquarters and three of the Commando units had all been heavily attacked, each finding it extremely diffi-cult to hold their own. So far we—45 Commando—were the only unit which had not been committed, but it would have been foolish to have left our dominating knoll positions whilst the Brigade situation as a whole was so unstable.

Throughout the afternoon 6 Commando bore the brunt of the enemy's attack on the bridge area. Finally, in order to clarify the situation, and really 'sort out' the Germans, their commanding officer, Lieutenant-Colonel Lewis, ordered a Commando bayonet charge.

With grim determination the entire unit lined up and fixed bayonets. Then, to the sound of a hunting horn, they

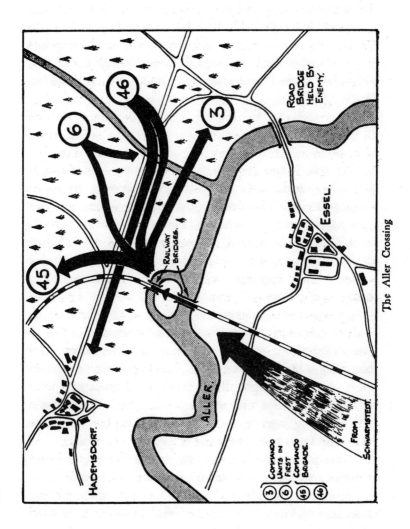

The Aller Crossing

charged, screaming and yelling as they rushed through the undergrowth towards the enemy.

It was a complete success. For over a quarter of a mile these men ran, routing all the Germans who stood before them. Some of the latter tried to make a stand, but in most cases they broke before such determined fury, to scatter in headlong flight.

3

By now it was obvious that there were over two companies of German infantry in the Aller Woods. Prisoners confirmed this. They told us that they belonged to a German Marine battalion which had been rushed from barracks in Wilhemshaven in an attempt to stem the eastward drive of British Second Army. The fact that we had clashed in the woods had been a pure coincidence. The Germans had been billeting there for the night. . . .

Meanwhile 46 Commando had managed to beat off the enemy attacks in their particular area, so that with 6 Commando's valiant efforts, the position everywhere was becoming a little more secure. The Brigadier now decided, as it was almost nightfall, to place the Brigade in a tight, all-round defensive ring until operations could be resumed the following morning. He accordingly withdrew us from our knoll to an area nearer the bridge : but we had not been in this new position very long before we were heavily counter-attacked by tanks and infantry.

The tanks nosed their way inquiringly down the main road leading towards the river. When they reached Charlie and Dog Troops' defences, however, they seemed so surprised at being fired on by PIATs at close range that they withdrew. The Wermacht infantry, seeing the strong arm of their assault wither so rapidly, beat a hasty retreat also.

The rest of the night passed without further incident. It was a period of considerable nervous strain for us, however, for we had never fought in country like this before, where every tree and bush seemed to resolve itself into a German soldier in the darkness, and where the crack of a twig might mean the stealthy foot of an advancing foe.

What the Germans did with themselves that night we never knew ; but we, for our part, were certainly not idle. Two companies of the K.S.L.I. were ferried across the river to the bridgehead under cover of darkness, and we heard from these Army lads as they quietly moved into their allotted positions that the pontoon bridge was nearly finished, and that the tanks of the Eleventh Armoured Division were waiting to cross.

4

At daybreak the next morning (April 12) we scrambled wearily from the depths of our slit trenches and stretched ourselves, standing up in the woods as we did so.

There was not a sign of the Germans. Everywhere was peaceful. The only sounds to be heard were the quiet crackle of our own breakfast fires, and the cautious tones of men talking amongst themselves as they hurried down to the river for a wash and shave. The hideous battle of the day before seemed an awful dream.

At seven o'clock orders came from Brigade headquarters to resume the attack. 45 and 46 Commandos, under the command of Lieutenant-Colonel T. M. Gray, were to advance through the woods, ' beating ' as they went for any signs of the enemy, towards the railway bridge. The main

road running due north through the wood was to be used
as the axis of advance, with 46 Commando ' beating ' along
the left-hand side in extended line, and ourselves moving
along on the right in similar fashion.

For this operation, we were told, we would probably
have the support of R.A.F. Typhoon aircraft, who would
attack known enemy targets beyond the railway bridge in
the vicinity of the village of Hademstorf—if they could be
spared for the job.

Half an hour later the advance commenced. All went
well until we approached the knoll which he had occupied on
the previous day: then we were greeted with a burst of
Spandau fire from the enemy, almost derisive in its abrupt-
ness. They had obviously infiltrated into our original
defences during the night.

Meanwhile 46 Commando had run into trouble in the
shape of hidden snipers and machine-guns on their side of
the road, too, which made it rather look as if the Germans
were proposing to stand along the entire front of our
advance.

For a good two hours both 46 Commando and ourselves
engaged the enemy, firing at them whenever we could see
them. This was no easy task, owing to the dense nature of
the woods, and the fact that the German infantry were
wearing camouflage jackets which blended admirably with
their surroundings.

Although the Mountain Gunner regiment supporting
us had been put ' on ' to the suspected enemy positions, and
were now harassing them with intense fire, it nevertheless
became obvious that neither Commando could possibly
advance until the knoll on our side of the road had been
cleared. Major Blake accordingly ordered Charlie Troop
to attack it: but within a few minutes of this Troop moving

forward of the Commando they ran into very heavy opposition, and in the course of the subsequent engagement suffered considerable casualties, including their Commander, Captain M. C. Brockbank, who was killed.

Whilst all this was going on the Typhoons arrived. They certainly were a godsend, for our position was now very awkward, to say the least, and we had only half-expected them in the first place. Roaring above our heads, they zoomed low over the woods, in rigid formation, heading unerringly for Hademstorf. A few seconds later we heard the screeching swish of rockets hurtling towards their targets ; then the Typhoons would turn and thunder back over our area. This performance was repeated two or three times, to the accompaniment of cheers from us as we lay flat on our bellies in the woods, shouting for joy between bouts of firing at the enemy.

Twenty minutes later the Typhoons finally departed, heading west in the morning sun towards their airstrip some miles behind the lines. As the fighting in the Aller Woods still continued as fruitlessly as ever, however—despite the R.A.F.'s timely intervention—Lieutenant-Colonel Gray decided that it was hopeless to continue without more detailed information as to the enemy's actual defences. 45 Commando and ourselves were accordingly withdrawn to the line of a canal running from east to west through the woods, about half a mile in rear.

Despite such a retreat the morning's work had not been entirely abortive. The few prisoners we had managed to capture revealed that, had it not been decided to beat through the woods towards the Schwarmstedt railway bridge that very morning, the entire Brigade would have been heavily attacked by the German Marine force concentrated in the railway bridge area. Apparently we had met these

gentlemen advancing towards us when we were beating up
to the knoll.

We spent another night in newly dug trenches—this
time in areas sited near the canal—and nothing happened.
There was just that awful feeling of pregnant stillness in the
woods, with their tall, dense clumps of trees, and the thick,
almost jungle-like scrub surrounding them.

The fighting had been more or less continuous for the
past forty-eight hours now. We began to wonder how it
would all end.

5

On the following morning—Friday, April 13—a reconnaissance patrol from Easy Troop, headed by Ian Beadle,
set out from the canal to investigate the knoll. They reached
it, to find no Germans there, and managed to get near
enough to the railway line to observe the enemy digging-in
just beyond it.

Patrols from 46 Commando also revealed activity by the
Germans in the vicinity of the railway, together with news
of an 88-millimetre gunsite to the north-west of our bridgehead. Acting on this information, Brigadier Mills-Roberts
ordered 45 Commando to move in strength up to the knoll,
whilst 46 Commando advanced to capture the village of
Hademstorf.

The operation commenced at eleven o'clock that morning. We reached our knoll without any trouble this time,
whilst 46 Commando, supported by a troop of 17-pounder
self-propelled guns, commenced the attack on Hademstorf.

The plan for the capture of this village was to deploy
four fighting Troops in a wide pincer movement—two
Troops going round on each flank. On the left flank of

their attack, however, 46 ran into a lot of trouble, and one of their fighting Troops was very badly cut about. Meanwhile, on the right flank, the other two Troops made a wide detour and, with great dash and speed, entered the village with hardly any opposition. On their way in they saw large numbers of the enemy running for all they were worth up the railway line to the north-east. The Troops of 46 engaged them with fire from the rear, and inflicted numerous casualties. The remainder of the Commando then marched into Hademstorf unopposed, and by midday the village was theirs.

6

So ended the battle of the Aller Woods. It had been a bitter three-day period of fighting, and although threatened with annihilation at first, the Brigade had eventually succeeded in scoring a crushing victory over a numerically superior enemy, consisting of two German Marine battalions, a battalion from an S.S. Panzer Division, and a Wermacht anti-tank unit armed with 88-millimetre guns.

By now the Aller itself had been successfully bridged, and already the tanks of the Eleventh Division—that famous division who bore as their emblem a black bull on a yellow field—had crossed, and were fanning out on the flat German plain which spread due east as far as the Elbe.

CHAPTER 14

PERIOD APRIL 18—APRIL 29, 1945

OUR Brigade remained spread over the Aller Woods and nearby Hademstorf for four days. Enemy resistance by now had completely collapsed, and prisoners straggling in from the outlying countryside told of Wermacht units lost and scattered over a considerable area, and who had been without food for over twenty-four hours.

On April 17 we were told that once more we were to be withdrawn into Corps reserve, acting as mobile flank protection force for the advance to the banks of the Elbe. From now on our moves were to be always at short notice like this, and we were destined never to remain more than a day or so in one place.

For the next forty-eight hours we drove rapidly across Germany in convoy, through the remnants of a score of towns and villages whose houses and principal buildings had been set on fire and reduced to smouldering shells by the tanks which preceded us. Of the German Army there was no sign. Often, too, as we headed east along dusty highways we would find ourselves held up for hours by unwieldy crowds of displaced persons, who had only just regained their freedom from the concentration camps, and in their thousands were making the most of it. They would pass us on carts, in stolen German cars (which seemed to run out of petrol all too soon) and on the backs of horses ; they drove cattle before them so that they could eat ; and on their backs were pots, pans, water bottles and old clothes. Every time

they met us they cheered in a dozen different tongues, and
when we looked at them closely we saw that they were little
more than walking skeletons, with ribs protruding pitifully
from their flesh, faces lined and haggard, and eyes that told
of a hundred sufferings.

2

On the 19th we entered the town of Luneberg, a beau-
tiful hospital town, some twelve miles west of the Elbe.
There was no fighting here, naturally enough, for thousands
of German wounded were convalescing, and the town had
been declared open.

Ahead of us now lay the Elbe, on which we knew the
German Army would try to make a last desperate stand
before being completely annihilated. However, it became
apparent that it would be some time before we could be
required to carry out an assault crossing of the river, and so
the Brigade made itself as comfortable as possible in Luneburg itself and the surrounding villages.

For the first time in weeks we enjoyed a really good, long
rest, with hot baths, good food and wine thrown in. The
wine we found in Luneberg was excellent. Most of us
billeted ourselves in the houses of German officers fighting
on the Russian front, and naturally their cellars were well
stocked with looted wines and liqueurs from various occupied countries.

It was our padre who claimed the honour of discovering
the best cellar in Luneberg. He asked the aged German frau
in whose house he was billeted if she had any wine one day,
and she replied very firmly that she hadn't. As he couldn't
find any in the house at the time he believed her.

A few days later, however, he decided to rummage through his bedroom. He went upstairs, to find the German frau busy at his wardrobe. As he entered the room she turned, and with a startled gasp, slammed the wardrobe door and stood in front of it.

Now the padre, who had a positive nose for wine, had not really investigated the contents of his wardrobe, since it seemed to contain, for the most part, women's clothes of an ancient and decidedly German character. This time, however, he knew that there was more in this article of furniture than met the eye. Politely but firmly, he moved the frau to one side, opened the wardrobe, to discover that it had no back to it. In actual fact it covered a large hole in the bedroom wall which led to a hitherto undiscovered room in the house.

Crawling through this hole the padre found treasure which exceeded his wildest dreams, for there, neatly stacked in crates, were magnums of champagne and bottle upon bottle of moselle, claret, burgundy, benedictine, cointreau and creme de menthe.

The padre gasped, sampled the contents of a bottle or two, then rushed off to inform Commando headquarters of his unholy find. Realising the game was up the German frau stifled her sobs of anger and walked stiffly from the room.

3

All in all, we spent ten very happy days in Luneberg. Apart from the obvious delights which the padre's treasure-trove had to offer, everything possible was organised by Brigade headquarters for our amusement. Football matches between units were arranged, cinemas were opened (show-

ing British films) and even E.N.S.A. arrived. To cap it all,
Colonel Gray arrived back from England to take over command of the unit once more. We were all very pleased to
have him back once again, and Major Blake, who had held
the fort as C.O. during his absence, reverted to second-in-
command of the unit. His had been a difficult task, for he
had had to assume command just after the Rhine crossing,
remaining as temporary C.O. throughout the bitter fighting
on the Weser and Aller.

In the meantime planning was going on for the assault
crossing of the Elbe. The name given to this operation was
' Operation Enterprise,' and First Commando Brigade, under
command of 15th (Scottish) Division were to cross the river
in two squadrons of Buffaloes, landing to form a small beach-
head some two miles downstream from the town of Lauenburg. At the same time 15th (Scottish) Division's 44th
Brigade would land to form a separate beach-head a mile or
so on our left, opposite the village of Artlenburg.

' Operation Enterprise ' was, in fact, to be a miniature
Rhine crossing. Lauenburg would be bombed by the R.A.F.
before we went in, and on the day after we had landed, a
Brigade of parachutists would drop beyond our beach-head
and link up with us. There would also be the usual immense
artillery support.

For a variety of reasons, however, neither the bombing
raid nor the airborne landing were put into effect. As it
turned out, they weren't required.

The detailed plan for our Brigade was as follows: 6
Commando were to land first and seize a beach-head,
followed by 46 Commando, who would lead the night infiltration—laying a white tape as they went—into Lauenberg.
The remaining units (3 Commando and ourselves) would
bring up the rear, together with Brigade headquarters.

As far as the enemy's defences were concerned, they
certainly had the advantage. Lauenburg lay at the top of
steep, almost sheer cliffs, one hundred and fifty feet high,
on the top of which the Germans had dug a series of trench
systems, reinforced with machine-gun posts ; and this was
not all, for just on the outskirts of Lauenburg itself, dominating all likely crossing-points on the river, was a battery of
40-millimetre anti-aircraft guns which, fired at low angle,
could rake and sink our craft as they went across.

4

At six o'clock on the evening of April 28 we marched
out of our billets in Luneburg to embus in transport waiting
on the main road leading towards the river.

The German civilians watched us leave in silence. They
knew that something was ' on '—probably the crossing of
the Elbe, but they weren't quite sure. In any case, there
wasn't much hope for Germany now.

We moved up in convoy to the concentration area on
the west bank of the Elbe at a crawling rate, and as we
drove through the various tiny villages which lay dotted
all over the flat country leading up to the river we could see
something of the preparations which were being made for
the night's offensive. Brawny artillerymen, their bodies
sweating with their exertions, were piling up great stores
of shells near their guns ; light anti-aircraft batteries were
being cleaned and trained on to their first targets ; and on
the road we were moving on, two long columns of Scottish
troops marched in single file.

At eight o'clock we finally reached the concentration
area. It was dark by this time, and we de-bussed on the

roadside in the usual fashion, scattering ourselves quickly
into small groups in the surrounding fields.

For the first hour nothing happened. Everyone was
lying down, trying to snatch what sleep they could ; and
then, at nine o'clock, our artillery opened up their 'softening'
programme on the known enemy defences.

It was like the Rhine all over again. The rumble of
heavy guns heralded the shrill whine of shells hissing through
the air towards selected targets, and once more the sky was
filled with a fantastic pattern of orange-coloured lights as
ack-ack shells ' pepper-potted ' Lauenburg. Already the
town was begininng to glow ominously as one building after
another caught fire.

Unlike the troops who had opposed us on the Rhine,
however, the German forces on the far side of the Elbe
proved to be foes of some spirit. Almost as soon as our own
artillery opened up they replied with a bombardment which,
if nothing like as heavy as ours, was at least disconcerting,
insomuch as the German gunners seemed to have guessed our
probable concentration area with some accuracy.

The noise of the shelling awakened everyone, and
Colonel Gray ordered the unit to commence digging-in where
they were.

As we unstrapped our entrenching tools from our belts
and started to make the first rough scrabbles in the earth,
the heavens suddenly opened to give us a shower of slow,
drizzling rain which steadily soaked through our equipment
and battledresses as we dug.

5

At ten o'clock a tremendous explosion was heard above
the roar of gunfire. Our engineers had blown two holes in

the steep flood bank, which would allow the Buffaloes free access to the river when the time to cross came.

For the next four hours both the shelling and the rain continued unabated. We lay in the bottoms of our shallow trenches, carved out in the darkness, meanwhile, and waited for the time to move.

At two o'clock in the morning the order finally came. We rose from our trenches to embark in the Buffaloes, as we had done on the Rhine five weeks before. 6 and 46 Commandos had already crossed and we could hear, very faintly, above the roar of the Buffaloes' engines, the crackle of tommy-gun fire and the whining burst of grenades.

For us the crossing over the Elbe was comparatively uneventful. There was not a lot of opposition from the enemy, apart from an occasional burst of Spandau bullets, or an odd shell from the ack-ack battery on the cliffs, all of which whined harmlessly enough above our heads. Elsewhere, however, the Germans were engaging one of the Brigade's units in the most intense fashion with one of their ack-ack guns. We could hear its rapid coughing noise as we neared the eastern bank.

With a grinding sound the Buffaloes suddenly touched down on the shingle, and within a matter of seconds everyone was piling out, with the massive cliffs looming up in front of them not ten yards inland.

We started to climb. The rain had not made matters any easier for us, for there was only one track, winding its way tortuously to the top, and this was muddy and slippery. We all wondered how 6 Commando had managed to scale the cliffs, fighting their way up, with an entrenched enemy hurling grenades down upon them.

After twenty minutes' hard climbing we finally reached the top, where the white tape which 46 Commando had

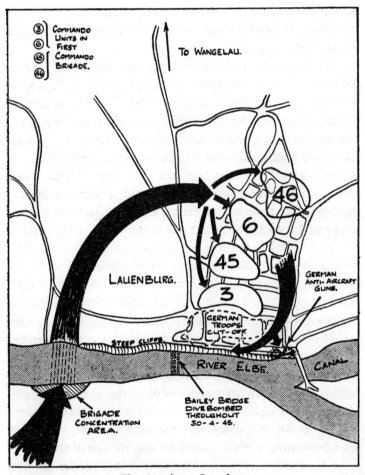

The Assault on Lauenburg

laid gleamed unmistakably in the darkness. As we raced
along this thin white strip a straggler from 46 told us what
had happened to the leading elements of the Brigade as they
fought their way ashore.

Despite the heavy artillery barrage which had been put
down by our Gunners, both 6 and 46 Commandos had run
into considerable opposition on landing, small-arms fire and
light ack-ack guns being brought to bear on them from both
flanks of the beach-head by the enemy. Stick grenades had
also been thrown in considerable numbers from the top of
the cliffs, causing numerous casualties, and when the two
units had finally reached the summit to commence the infiltration into Lauenburg, an enemy mortar, firing from
seemingly nowhere, had opened up and, purely by chance,
landed some bombs right amongst the ' snake ' of men as
they were forming up.

6

For the remainder of that night the town of Lauenburg
was slowly but surely occupied by a steady, unending stream
of men who (as they had done on the Rhine) moved in to
secure previously determined objectives, the occupation of
which would trap the enemy within the town and deny
them any chance of escape.

By daybreak Lauenburg was virtually ours. We had
captured our objectives, and there was no sign of the enemy
—at least as far as our particular unit was concerned. 46
Commando, apparently, found numbers of the enemy
digging-in near them, both sides being completely unaware
of the other's presence. The Germans, however, when they
saw the men of 46, gave in without a fight.

The whole of the town was now believed to be clear of the enemy, with the exception of the light ack-ack battery at the top of the cliffs overlooking the Elbe ; and Baker Troop were now ordered by Colonel Gray to advance and capture these German positions.

Moving off under command of John Day, the Troop closed to within one hundred yards of the battery. At this stage the Germans suddenly opened up, spraying the road and surrounding buildings with a vicious fusilade of 37-millimetre shells. Baker Troop immediately scattered for cover, and the whole street became alive with orange-coloured flashes as the shells smacked and roared into the already shattered fabric of blasted buildings.

The men of Baker Troop crouched low behind what cover they could find, awaiting the order to move forward and assault the battery. Meanwhile, as John Day started to shout preliminary orders above the roar of gunfire, a young Scots Bren-gunner, Marine Norman Towler, got to his feet and coolly returned the enemy fire from an exposed position.

For some unknown reason the Germans suddenly stopped firing. Perhaps they were too flabbergasted by Towler's action to continue : but whatever their reason, it made them lose the day, for Baker Troop seized the initiative and rushed the battery. Within minutes the guns had all been overrun, and something like fifty prisoners rounded up, including some German W.A.A.F.s, who emerged coyly from a series of dug-outs.

7

The war against Germany was almost over. The British Army had overcome all obstacles, and before them lay a

clear road to the Baltic. Soon the Elbe would be bridged,
and the tanks crossing, to stream in long columns across
Schleswig-Holstein. It would not be long, either, before
a link-up with the mighty Russian Armies—now reported
to be fighting in Berlin—would be effected.

Chapter 15

PERIOD APRIL 30—MAY 8, 1945

Throughout the afternoon of April 29 enemy aircraft had become more and more active in their efforts to hinder the men of the Royal Engineers who were trying to bridge the Elbe. This was the first time our Brigade had seen enemy planes since the Normandy campaign, and it was rather surprising how they managed to operate at this stage in the war, considering the fact that nearly the whole of North-West Germany was now in Allied hands.

The planes came in singly, carrying one bomb apiece, at half-hour intervals, and we identified them as Stukas, Focke-Wulfe 190s, and Messerschmitt 109s.

Flying very low over the river, with anti-aircraft guns of every type putting up a tremendous barrage against them from the western bank, and with our own men firing the newly captured 40-millimetre battery from Lauenburg, the dive-bombers came screaming in, releasing their bombs just before they passed over the bridge, then climbing steeply into the sun, to disappear from view.

Fortunately they did not succeed in hitting the bridge once, although they seriously hindered convoys that were trying to cross, not to mention the tanks, who by this time were fretting impatiently at the prospect of losing precious time before starting their ' swan ' to the Baltic. By four o'clock in the afternoon, however, the situation had become noticeably quieter, and as evening drew on the attacks ceased altogether.

We slept peacefully that night, and awoke next morning to find the Elbe bridged, with elements of the Eleventh Armoured and Sixth Airborne Divisions already crossing. Meanwhile Brigadier Mills-Roberts issued orders that all Commandos were to stand by for a further advance: but although we waited in readiness throughout the morning, it was not until two o'clock in the afternoon that the final order to move came.

Still carrying out the role of flank protection force to the main axis of 8 Corps' advance, the Brigade task this time was to move east in the wake of the Eleventh Armoured Division, clearing villages and small towns which might hold ' pockets ' of enemy troops in the process. The specific villages allotted to our Commando in the first phase of this advance were those of Lutau and Wangelau which lay some twelve and fifteen miles due east of Lauenburg respectively.

Punctually at two o'clock we moved off in transport from Lauenburg, and about a mile and a half from Lutau— now a smoking ruin, thanks to our Gunners—de-bussed from the convoy to advance into the village on foot. As the leading element of our Commando crept cautiously in, however, they found that Lutau had already been cleared by a Scottish infantry battalion. Colonel Gray immediately issued instructions for the advance to continue to Wangelau, the unit moving across country on the left flank of the village, which would be cleared and occupied until such time as further orders were received from the Brigadier.

It was not known whether there were any German troops in Wangelau or not, and as it was best never to take chances we accordingly moved with the same caution as had been exercised before entering Lutau. Easy Troop, under

Ian Beadle, led the way, and we advanced, the usual long, single file, down hedgerows and the edges of woods, along narrow tracks between fields, until we finally came within sight of Wangelau, marching stealthily now along a country lane which entered the village from the west.

We were still some two miles from our objective, and although no signs of the enemy had been observed so far, it did not necessarily mean that there weren't any in the immediate vicinity, for the country we were moving through would have been ideal for an ambush.

About a mile from the village Ian Beadle suddenly halted his Troop, and we all went to ground straight away. A minute or so later a runner came back to Colonel Gray to tell him that large numbers of Germans had been seen marching through Wangelau, carrying weapons.

Coloney Gray called up the Gunners on his radio, and told them to stand by. The advance into Wangelau continued.

2

One hundred yards from the outskirts of the village Ian Beadle halted his Troop again, sending one section forward to investigate a large farm on the right-hand side of the lane. The section entered the farmyard unopposed, then climbed through the farmhouse windows to see what was going on inside. To their surprise they found a large party of S.S. officers and men calmly sitting down to a meal. For a split second there was a deathly hush: then the men of Easy Troop acted. With a roar of ' *Handes hoch !* ' they leaped into the room. The S.S. men offered no fight. They dropped everything and stood up where they were, hands in the air. . . .

Meanwhile, the remainder of Easy Troop moved into the farmyard area also, and without any fighting whatsoever captured another party of the enemy in the kitchen of the farmhouse. The latter were busy cooking themselves a meal at the time, which Easy Troop proceeded to sit down and enjoy.

All the prisoners were passed back to Commando headquarters. Easy Troop then took up defensive positions beyond the farmhouse, on both sides of the lane, behind a low wall overlooking the village green, waiting for any further signs of the Germans before proceeding to clear the rest of the village.

A few minutes later a third party of the enemy were observed marching into Wangelau—from the north—with their packs on their backs, and their weapons at the ready. When they reached the edge of the village green all hell was let loose as Easy Troop's Bren guns and rifles were opened up on them.

The startled Germans, who had been well and truly ambushed, dropped where they were. Those who had not been hit ran for the cover of nearby farms and cottages, and once they were inside commenced to return our fire.

For the next twenty minutes bullets were exchanged at spasmodic intervals by both sides. Meanwhile, Colonel Gray moved up Able Troop to occupy the houses on the right of Ian Beadle's men, and the Gunners put down a heavy concentration on the enemy, who had by now grouped themselves at the northern end of the village.

The air was filled with the chatter of Spandau and Bren fire, broken only by the vicious crumping noise of exploding shells. When the Gunners' concentration finally lifted the Germans—possibly realising that they had run into far more trouble than they originally suspected—ceased firing and proceeded to poke several dirty-looking white handkerchiefs through the windows of their houses.

It was not really wise to trust them. Their white flags had been displayed in the most half-hearted manner. Perhaps they wanted to entice us into the open with this surrender offer, then shoot us down. We had been caught like this before. After some debate on the subject, we eventually decided to take a chance. A section of Easy Troop moved forward into the open, crossed the village green, and advanced towards the German-occupied houses, covered by the guns of their comrades from behind the farmyard wall.

To our surprise—and relief—the Germans really meant to surrender, and within half an hour we had rounded up something like 135 prisoners. The day was ours; but it had not been won entirely without casualties to ourselves. One man had been killed—Sergeant Jock Wilson, of Easy Troop, by a stray German rifle bullet. He was the last of us to die in action.

3

Meanwhile, the remainder of the Brigade had advanced to clear several villages to the south and east of Wangelau. The German Army, as a fighting machine at least, was now completely finished. Within forty-eight hours of our occupying Wangelau, tank formations of the British Second Army had reached the Baltic without encountering any opposition.

But the war was not completely over. On the following morning we saw a lone aircraft duel fought in the clear, sunny sky between a Spitfire and a Messerschmitt, right above our heads. All of us cheered madly as the Messerschmitt was finally shot to earth, a madly careering comet, beplumed with flames.

It crashed a mile or so east of the village, and when we sent out a party to look at it we found the usual gruesome wreckage of a fuselage, with the pilot lying a few yards away from his machine, a battered mass of flesh. We took his identification papers from him, then buried him. His name was Kohler, and his rank was Sergeant-Major in the Luftwaffe.

During the afternoon we buried Sergeant Wilson, too. It seemed an ironical twist of fate that these two men, one British and the other German, should die almost as the last shots of the war being fired. To us it symbolised the stupidity of the whole business.

We laid Sergeant Wilson to rest in the shadow of the farmhouse where he had fought his last battle, not so very far away from the grave of Kohler.

4

On the following morning (May 1) the Brigade commenced to move up to the Baltic. By this time the Sixth Airborne Division had made contact with elements of the Russian Army, and the final surrender could only be a matter of days.

As we headed north-east in convoy on that last advance it became increasingly evident to us how the German people had exhausted both themselves and their resources in six years of war. Everywhere bore signs of the complete and utter defeat of a misguided nation. The bombed and shell-torn houses; the trails of wrecked tanks and Wermacht transport, lying grotesquely on roadsides and in ditches; the never-ending columns of weary, travel-stained prisoners, marching, always marching, to the surrender points; the look of apathy and bewilderment on the faces of the people themselves.

On May 2 we arrived in Neustadt, a small Baltic port twelve miles north of the great German city of Lubeck, which had been 8 Corps' final objective in the campaign. We did not expect any resistance, and we did not encounter any. Our orders were simply to occupy the town, which we did without any bother at all, securing the usual comfort' able billets into the bargain.

Neustadt, superficially a port whose trade had been crippled by war, proved in reality to be a hothouse of enemy atrocities. A concentration camp was found down at the docks, grossly overcrowded with prisoners of all nationali' ties, all of whom had been forced to exist on little or no food, and had been subjected to very cruel treatment by their German captors. Several ' hell'ships,' containing hundreds of political prisoners, most of them dead or dying, were also discovered in the harbour : but the German people, when questioned about these matters, professed complete ignorance.

We stayed in Neustadt for six days, during which time the various areas to be occupied by the Commando units in the Brigade were drawn up. The particular area allotted to us was Kreis* Eutin, a portion of Schleswig-Holstein about the size of Northumberland.

5

On the night of May 7 news that the war was over reached us. Somehow we did not feel particularly elated. We had had a job to do, and we had done it. An even

* The equivalent of a county in Britain.

greater job awaited us, for on the morrow—VE Day—
we would be moving into Kreis Eutin to begin our occupation duties.

A lot of us thought about all the different things that
had happened to us since that day, nearly a year before,
when we had touched down on the beaches of Normandy.
So many things had happened, so many battles fought, so
many men lost, so much ground covered ; and now, here we
were, a collection of men drawn from all walks of life, on
our final objective—to use a military phrase. We had been
borne on the shrill wind of war across a Continent. Our
banner had been unfurled and carried before us, the banner
which all of us inwardly carried in our hearts, the banner
which so clearly stated what we thought was right, and what
was wrong. . . .

VE Day dawned, and we moved by convoy into Eutin,
principal town of the Kreis. As the trucks rumbled into the
square the German people watched us, their faces a study
of mixed emotion—fear, apprehension, despair, contempt,
hatred, apathy, pity.

The British occupation of Germany had begun.

POSTSCRIPT

OVER 40 years have passed since this book was first written. During that time 45 Royal Marine Commando has served in virtually every theatre in which Britain has had some form of military involvement.

When the Army Commandos were disbanded after the Second World War a single Royal Marines Commando Brigade was formed, comprising 40, 42 and 45 RM Commandos. Each Commando operated independently or in conjunction with other formations, as and when required, and continues to do so.

From 1946 to 1967, spanning three decades, 45 Commando was based continuously overseas. It served in Hong Kong and Palestine, engaged in anti-terrorist campaigns in Malaysia, Cyprus and Aden, undertook peace-keeping duties when troubles arose in Kuwait and East Africa. It also made history when, for the 1956 invasion of Suez, it became the first military unit ever to make an opposed landing by helicopter.

Following its return to Britain at the end of the 1960s, the Commando took up other duties including spells of service in Northern Ireland. At the same time, in the great tradition of the Royal Marines, it stood trained and prepared to move quickly, as a 'fire-fighting force', to any other part of the world.

This high degree of readiness was put fully to the test in the early months of 1982, when the Falklands crisis arose—and where Royal Marines were already serving. Together with 49 and 42 Commandos and men of the Parachute Regiment, the Brigade of Guards, the Ghurhkas and other formations, 45 Commando helped to make up the highly professional fighting force which, after being transported 7,000 miles south from Britain to the edge of Antarctica, successfully fought and defeated a greatly superior Argentine army in terms of numbers—and took 9,000 prisoners in the process.

Today, 45 Commando is a spearhead unit specialising in Arctic warfare. Based in Scotland, its principal role is to guard NATO's northern flank in Norway. But it also remains, as ready as ever, to serve at short notice wherever it may be needed.

Bryan Samain
1988